The Battle of Lynchburg

Seize Lynchburg— If Only For A Single Day!

L. VanLoan Naisawald

Foreword by James I. Robertson, Jr.

The Battle of Lynchburg:
Seize Lynchburg—If Only for a Day!

ISBN: 1890306681

Library of Congress Control Number: 2004104496

Cover painting by Don Troiani, www.historicalartprints.com

WARWICK HOUSE PUBLISHING
720 Court Street
Lynchburg, VA 24504
(434) 846-1200

FOREWORD

Local history is the seed from which a national heritage grows. Regionalism has made America what it is. At the same time, every citizen should feel an obligation to look back whence he or she came. History is but the ground on which we walk. Being familiar with where we have been is the surest way to face with confidence where we are going.

In 1860 Lynchburg, Virginia was a vibrant town of both prosperity and promise. Situated in the center of Virginia's rolling piedmont country, the town's 7,000 residents could boast of strong connections with the rest of the state. The business district was alongside the majestic James River. Through the downtown ran the James River and Kanawha Canal, the major commercial line from the Shenandoah Valley to Richmond and beyond. The Virginia and Tennessee Railroad provided another east-west artery, while the Orange and Alexandria rail line began at Lynchburg and snaked to within sight of Washington. Six roads converged on Lynchburg from all directions.

Such transportation facilities turned Lynchburg into a trade center. Tobacco was the community's base. Fifteen tobacco warehouses were spread throughout the city. In addition, four iron foundries, eleven gristmills, and smaller businesses all gave Lynchburg much more in common with industrialized Richmond than with farming communities such as Danville.

That extraordinary transportational and commercial network gave Lynchburg quick and increased recognition when civil war exploded over the land. As the largest city in central Virginia, Lynchburg immediately became a vital connecting link in state resources as well as military strategy. The city was a natural site for army rendezvous camps. During the war years, storage warehouses along the railroads and canal were in constant use. The "Hill City" became one of the largest military medical centers west of Richmond and one of only two locales for the treatment of diseased and crippled horses.

Not until 1864 were Union forces in a position to make Lynchburg a principal target. A major Federal effort got underway in June. Whether the results came from Southern valor, Union incompetence, or both, the Lynchburg Campaign deserves far more attention than it has received. The stakes on both sides were high, for the safety of Richmond and the existence of Confederate Virginia hung in the balance during the two days of maneuvering and fighting in and around the city.

The Lynchburg Campaign is an exciting story, filled with colorful personalities, dramatic actions, and a string of might-have-beens. As with great battles of history, the Lynchburg engagement has its unresolved controversies. History is—and should be—the most exciting subject of learning because it is the living chronicle of human beings in action. A prime example lies in this book.

L. VanLoan Naisawald has long been recognized as a leading military historian of the Civil War. His principal work, *Grape and Canister: The Story of the Field Artillery in the Army of the Potomac, 1861-1865*, remains forty years after its publication a basic source on the Civil War's big guns. Naisawald's residency in Lynchburg sparked an interest in the campaign for the city. This book is a product of deep research, judicious analyses, and obvious love for one's adopted town. That is a near ideal blend of writing ingredients.

This is a publication of recently established Historic Sandusky. Named for the estate that was Union headquarters during the 1864 campaign, this association of Lynchburg-area residents is working hard to uncover and preserve what many would term the most important era in the city's long, proud history.

Our Civil War resolved fundamental questions about the American union. In doing so, it created a single nation that has become the leader of the world. This badly needed volume tells of one vital step in the evolution of the United States.

James I. Robertson, Jr.

TABLE OF CONTENTS

PREFACE

The creation of Historic Sandusky Foundation in 2000 filled a void in preserving the history of Lynchburg in the Civil War. Now for the first time there is a focal point for the study of the events of that day as well as being the starting point for a self-guided auto tour of Civil War Lynchburg with the battle narrated by the well-known Civil War authority, Dr. James I. "Bud" Robertson.

Additionally, a videotape about the battle, narrated by the eminent Civil War historian Ed Bearrs, is under development. Both of these will be available for sale at Sandusky.

The Sandusky mansion itself is to undergo physical restoration that will include a museum, displays, and maps focusing on the city and its environs of that time as well as the engagement itself. At significant dates there will be public programs highlighting the Civil War history in Lynchburg.

It follows, then, that there should be a suitable up-to-date published account of the engagement itself to accompany the driving tape and the video presentation. This book is the result.

CHAPTER 1

A Fat Prize It Would Be

The little wood-burning engine, spewing clouds of dirty smoke, chugged slowly southward, then rattled across the James River trestle into the city of Lynchburg. Behind it clattered some cars jammed with Confederate troops. Easing slowly into the station tracks beside the river's edge and the adjacent James River and Kanawha Canal, the train squeaked to a stop. On the train, probably in the cab of the engine, a Confederate general quickly plopped on his head his wide, white-brimmed felt hat, characteristically turned up on the right side, and stepped down from the cab. Looking about, the general yelled for his horse. An aide scurried to one of the cars and off-loaded the general's mount. Gen. Jubal A. Early and the lead elements of the famed II Corps of the Army of Northern Virginia, the Corps once led by the redoubtable Stonewall Jackson, was arriving to save the city of Lynchburg from the approaching Yankees. It was sometime around 1:00 p.m., June 17, 1864, and the citizens of Lynchburg were now exuberant.But could the city be saved?[1]

Just five days earlier on June 12 at 3:00 a.m., Early had been called to General Lee's headquarters near Richmond, where he was given verbal orders to prepare to move his Corps to save Lynchburg. Then, at 3:00 a.m. on the 13th, written confirmation arrived! With just over 8,000 men and twenty-four cannon of two artillery battalions under Gen. Armistead L. Long, the Corps left the lines near Richmond and began the long, hard four-day march toward Charlottesville and a railhead there, almost one hundred miles distant. Unfortunately for the Confederates, Sheridan's troopers had just torn up the rail lines between there and Charlottesville so a road march was necessary. It was a tired Corps that took up the march; it had been fighting almost constantly since early May, terrible battles that had taken it through the Wilderness and Spotsylvania and on to Cold Harbor. But it was still a cocky body of men that headed out following what is today Route 250. [2]

At some point in the march Early rode ahead, reaching the railroad depot at Keswick, six miles east of Charlottesville, some time in the early morning of June 16th. There he received a telegram from Gen. John C. Breckinridge in Lynchburg, telling him that a Union army under a Gen. David Hunter was closing dangerously on that city, having reached the village of Liberty, today called Bedford, barely twenty-five miles southwest of the city.[3] The II Corps was urgently needed. But Early was a good sixty miles away to oppose Hunter and his army of 18,000 men. The degree of urgency was obvious; a fast troop movement by rail was the answer.

Jubal A. Early

There is an interesting account of Early's actions shortly after his Charlottesville arrival on the morning of June 16th. Here, according to the memoirs of Colonel William Allan, Early came upon several old friends, among whom was former Congressman Shelton Leake. The former Congressman offered the tired general a drink, which he promptly accepted. This was followed by another, and then another, until by noon, Old Jube was beginning to show his liquor, the only time Colonel Allan reported that he ever saw him so affected! Finally, later that afternoon Early's extremely able adjutant, Sandie Pendleton, who had also been Stonewall Jackson's adjutant, persuaded him to go to the home of Professor Albert Bledsoe, who had invited him to tea. That evening Sandie and Colonel Allan returned to find the general "entirely himself" and hard at work arranging for the move of his troops by rail to Lynchburg.[4]

However, it was not until some time well after dark on the 16th that the leading elements of the II Corps marched into the Keswick Station. In Early's 1866 account, *A Memoir of the Last Year of The War for Independence*, some time after he arrived in Keswick, he located a train of the Virginia Central line that was scheduled to leave for Waynesboro. He immediately commandeered it and at 11:40 a.m. telegraphed Breckinridge in Lynchburg (who had just reached that city on the 16th) asking that all available Orange and Alexandria engines and cars in Lynchburg be sent to him. Again, at 12:30 p.m. an anxious Early wired Breckinridge to send all available engines and cars in that city to him immediately; seize engines and cars from both the Virginia Central and the Orange and Alexandria lines there, threatening all with dire results for failure to respond promptly. He demanded prompt action and he would assume complete responsibility. But things moved slowly. At 2:20 p.m. still no trains had arrived, and he again wired Breckinridge that he could not start until cars reached him. Breckinridge was to prod the railroad superintendent; Early had had experience with the superintendent and didn't trust him. However, if the railroads responded promptly all would be well.[5]

Additionally, orders went to his commanders Gen. Stephen D. Ramseur and Gen. John B. Gordon to hold themselves in readiness; they would be the first to load when trains became available. Gen. Robert E. Rodes' division, the rest of Gordon's division, and artillery would march by road until railroad trains could be provided. General Rodes, whose home was in Lynchburg, protested vigorously. He felt he and his division had priority due to their knowledge of the country and the desire to defend his home town. Early stubbornly said no and the order stood.

At some point either late on the 16th or early on the 17th General Early acquired some trains—six by one account,[6] however, none of these were ready, he wrote, until sunrise of the 17th. But by that time he had enough transportation to move Ramseur's division and one brigade of Gordon's. Loading of these troops began at dawn—and Early himself climbed aboard the first train, probably the commandeered one. He then wired Breckinridge at 7:40 a.m. that he was on his way with an expected arrival time between 12:00 and 1:00

p.m. But, he added, the railroads were slow. The remainder of the tired men of the Corps that had been fighting constantly for over a month would wearily answer the command to fall in and resume their marching on the 17th, tramping alongside the tracks until cars could return and pick them up, probably at North Garden south of Charlottesville.

Among the units loading that day was the famous Stonewall Brigade. As the train carrying the unit reached the James River at Lynchburg and began entering the covered bridge there, the rear car jumped the track. Immediately yells pierced the air as troops screamed at the engineer to stop, fearing the entire train might suddenly be dumped into the river. Men started jumping off. Some landed on the timbers of the trestle and were badly hurt. One or two were killed outright. The train stopped, and frantically the disabled car was uncoupled and pushed over the trestle into the river, then the trip into the depot resumed. Little time was wasted as the troops

At far left is a covered railroad bridge (c. 1880) over the James River. It is similar to if not the original of 1864. In the foreground is a canal packet such as used to move the VMI cadets to Lynchburg from near Glasgow. These and other river craft also carried vital supplies by canal from Lynchburg to Richmond. Photo courtesy The Library of Virginia.

During the Civil War, troops were often moved by rail, crammed within and atop the cars. This scene is similar to that which greeted Early's men as they arrived at Lynchburg.

detrained and were formed amid the cheers and shouts of the local citizenry who heaped food and drink upon them. In short time they were quickly marched out to the city fairgrounds. A confident Early wired Richmond that he had arrived with sufficient strength to secure the city.[7]

To the waiting and frightened people of Lynchburg, the sight of this first trainload of troops, perhaps some 600 lean, lanky battle-hardened veterans unloading in front of their eyes, sent spirits soaring. One account by a Confederate veteran of that campaign, Milton Humphreys, in his *History of the Lynchburg Campaign*, remarked that the troops were cheered constantly, bands played, and ladies came down to hand out lunches and cool water. One of the most famous parts of Gen. Robert E. Lee's army—Early and the renown II Corps, formerly that of the legendary Stonewall Jackson, were now arriving to face the Union Army approaching Lynchburg. These citizen demonstrations reportedly went on all night and into the next day as trains rattled in and out of the depot.

But what the local citizenry failed to realize was that it would be many more hours before the full strength of the Corps arrived. Even today just exactly how many of Early's men arrived that day and when is not certain. In his 1866 account, Early wrote that though the first train arrived about 1:00 p.m., "other trains were much later." One of Ramseur's soldiers wrote that it was late afternoon when his unit arrived. Early also added that the track and the rolling stock were in bad condition.[8] It was a sixty-mile trip each way and the railroad was single track with an unknown number of pull-offs to allow an oncoming train to pass a returning one, thus making timing for returning trains questionable.

There is evidence that trains in the early 1860s could pull as many as ten cars, with each capable of carrying a total weight of 16,000 pounds. However, according to Dr. John Arnold of Lynchburg, a present day authority on Civil War railroad capabilities, worn engines of 1864 were capable of pulling no more than eight cars. Tom Ledford, administrator of the Lynchburg Museum and a railroad authority, also agrees with the figure of a maximum of eight cars, which he found in his investigation of contemporary train wrecks.

Troop train arriving in Lynchburg

No more than about seventy-five men could be loaded aboard and atop each car. Train speed at that time, according to Arnold, would not have been much more than twelve miles per hour, given the poor condition of the engines, the roadbed, the steep grades in spots and the fully loaded cars. Further, it was extremely risky to run trains in reverse for any distance. Such a method caused derailments, so the engines had to be turned around at Lynchburg.

Early states that both Ramseur's division and part of Gordon's arrived in time to be in position late that afternoon. Some time after that, perhaps even into mid-evening, the trains that had carried Ramseur's and part of Gordon's commands into the city now returned northward, one behind the other, to pick up the remainder of Gordon's and all of Rodes' commands. But Early did not expect these to arrive until the morning of the 18th[9] and the evidence is that these troops may not have arrived until late on the 18th, even though some of the units had marched a considerable distance that day and thus the pickup point for these troops was closer to Lynchburg than the initial pickup point of Keswick. George Morris and Susan Foutz in their book *Lynchburg In The Civil War* place the pickup spot as North Garden Depot, about twelve miles south of Keswick.

So the delay in bringing the remainder of the Corps was due to the jamming of the trains in the available depot space at Lynchburg and the single track back north again. According to Ledford, there was sufficient track siding space in the city depot to have held all six of the trains at the same time, as they arrived roughly end-to-end. But then there would have been a considerable delay in reversing the engines on the turntable there and then running them back serially to pick up the rest of the Corps. There may have been a turning switch system or turntable at Keswick or North Garden but certainly none closer to Lynchburg than that.

Considering then that the six-train figure was correct, the number of troops that arrived by the afternoon of the 18th, based on the estimate of cars per train and men per car, would have been 3,800—close to the figure of 4,000 cited by Humphreys. Therefore, with each division of Early's 8,000 man three-division Corps having the same strength, or 2,700 men, by late afternoon of the 18th the 2,700 men of Ramseur, plus perhaps a third of Gordon's or 900, gives a total of 3,600 or just under half of his entire Corps. Additionally were the 2,000 of Breckinridge's division, the 3,000-3,500 cavalry of both Imboden and McCausland, 250 VMI cadets, and 1,800 walking wounded and militia—a total of just over 11,000 men to face Hunter. But Early believed his reconnisance that on the afternoon of the 17th, Hunter had close to 20,000 men as he approached the city. It was, then, a very tenuous situation that Early would face on the afternoon of June 17th, but his combative nature added weight against the odds. Hopefully he could count on the remainder of Gordon's and all of Rodes' men to arrive by the next day, adding perhaps another 4,500 men to his combat strength, a total approximating 15,650.

This train scenario fits in with the oft-told legend that on the afternoon and evening of June 17th Early ran a switch engine and some empty cars in and out of the city, creating an impression to the Federals on the outskirts of town that reinforcements were pouring in to Early's ranks—which indeed they were. There certainly was a tremendous amount of noise all afternoon of the 17th, and much of that evening and night, with trains tooting horns, rattling over the bridge, engines being reversed and crowds cheering. But there were probably quiet times during which Early used his engine ploy to confound his enemy, the crowds continuing to cheer and make noise—with Early's encouragement. Whatever the source, the Federals heard the racket and believed Lynchburg was being heavily reinforced. But in retrospect, one cannot help but believe that had Hunter been more aggressive, he might well have seized the city before sufficient strength arrived to save it.

CHAPTER 2

Hunter Gets His Mission

The trigger that prompted Early on his sudden journey from near Richmond to Lynchburg was pulled by the northern military commander, Gen. Ulysses S. Grant. This general, called in from the western theater of operations, had taken command of all of the Federal armies in March 1864. He quickly determined that forceful concerted action by the far-flung Union armies, at multiple points, was the way to win this war. In early April 1864, Grant issued his orders to Gen. William T. Sherman, fighting in Georgia, to destroy the weaker Confederate forces there and then sever that quarter of the Confederacy from the heartland. In the process Sherman would leave the states of Georgia and South Carolina a wasteland[10] from whence no source of supply for the Confederacy could be gotten.

A second force, Gen. George G. Meade's veteran Army of the Potomac, operating in the eastern part of Virginia, would begin pounding away at Gen. Robert E. Lee's outnumbered Army of Northern Virginia. A third army, commanded by Gen. Franz Sigel, one of President Abraham Lincoln's miserable political appointees, was to drive southwestward up the Shenandoah Valley of Virginia, clearing it of Confederate forces. The Valley had been and still was the breadbasket for General Lee's Army of Northern Virginia. Its loss to the Southern cause would be truly traumatic. It was Grant's belief that under such combined pressure by these four armies, later augmented by Gen. Benjamin Butler's force below Richmond, each outnumbering their opposing foe, the Confederacy must certainly come to an end.

These offensives began simultaneously in early May 1864. Sherman began hammering at the smaller army of Gen. Joseph Johnston, commanded later by Gen. John B. Hood, and in the fall began his march to the sea. Grant accompanied Meade's army as it began slashing at Lee in central Virginia in the vicious battles that became known as the Wilderness Campaign. Over in the Shenandoah Valley Sigel had put together scattered commands and under his control began to drive southwestward toward the critical Confederate rail junction and supply base of Staunton. But in mid-May of 1864, at a small crossroads village called New Market, about forty miles north of Staunton, Sigel was humiliatingly defeated by Gen. John C. Breckinridge with a hastily thrown together smaller army that included a force of some 250 VMI cadets.

Grant and United States Secretary of War Edwin Stanton quickly removed Sigel from command. Stanton pushed for Gen. David Hunter as Sigel's replacement and wired Grant accordingly. Grant replied that he agreed with the necessity for change and to appoint "General Hunter or any one else to the command of West Virginia," as that position was then termed. So, in his place came fiery abolitionist David Hunter, a confidant of the Secretary of War and an acquaintance of President Lincoln. Grant's orders to Hunter were the same as Sherman's—destroy the enemy forces in the Valley and turn it into a wasteland. In early June, in response to his orders, Hunter began his drive to clear the Valley. His first objective was to destroy the Confederate army there, then seize the important railhead and supply base at Staunton, including all military related supplies and facilities in the surrounding areas as well.

General David Hunter

But once the Confederate forces in the valley had been destroyed, Grant's message-order gave Hunter the option of moving eastward over the Blue Ridge to Charlottesville, destroying railroads as he went; or should the order reach Hunter after he had begun a march up the

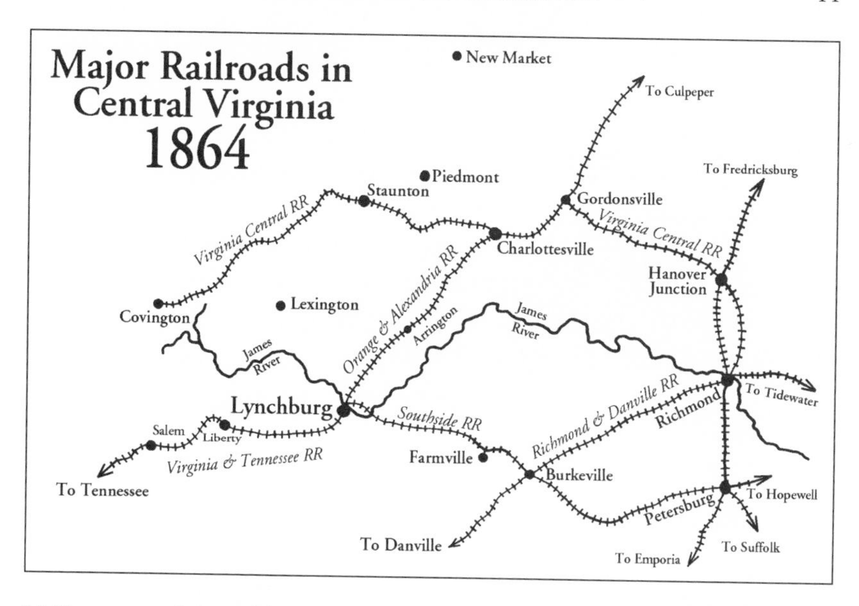

Valley toward Lynchburg, he was to continue toward that city, with its vital Confederate supply and rail center in south central Virginia. At that time Lynchburg was the second largest city in the state, a city of some 7,000, of which about half were slaves and free blacks. There three railroads and a large canal system combined to forward supplies of every kind to Lee's army facing Grant and Meade. Grant saw the canal system of such value that he mentioned it twice in his order as worthy of destruction.[11] Lynchburg was truly an immense and busy supply center. In the city were supplies of grain and fodder; much needed salt for curing; lead from the mines to the southwest for ammunition; four iron foundries; an ammunition factory; a military clothing factory; eleven grist mills; a railroad maintenance and repair shop; food supplies in a variety of types; warehouses with arms and ammunition; a foundry that repaired cannon; and a number of small businesses making or repairing harness as well as wagons and caissons.[12]

Further, every large building in the city had wounded Confederate soldiers moving in and out—many hobbling or swathed in bandages, for the city had become the second largest military hospital complex in the Confederacy. Some nineteen big tobacco factories and thirteen other buildings had been converted to hospitals to house the thousands of sick and wounded arriving daily from the battlefields to the

The two surviving former tobacco warehouses that served as part of the vast Confederate General Hospital System in Lynchburg.

east. (Today only two of the tall, beautiful brick tobacco buildings still stand.) Lynchburg was indeed a rich prize almost ready for the picking. Grant saw the city's value to the Confederacy for he wired Hunter that the complete destruction of the railroad system there, along with the canal, "is of great importance to us...it would be of great value to us to get possession of Lynchburg for a single day."

For three years the city had escaped the ravages of war. A letter from a wounded Confederate soldier recovering in the city that June of 1864 told of the city and its unbelievable affluence. He called it a "great city … instead of a city of 7 hills it is at least on 70." The soldier found the people industrious and one was able to purchase anything there that "could be had at NY." The stores were full and food was plentiful and the ladies all extremely well dressed in silk, satin and broadcloth. And all that summer he reported that he never suffered for want of food. But for almost a week in mid-June 1864, the heretofore-untouched city had a strong case of the jitters as Hunter and his marauding army closed on it with seeming vengeance.

CHAPTER 3

The Federal Army's Cast of Characters

For three years, 1861-1863, the city of Lynchburg had been spared the crashing waves of combat against its gates. The eye of the storm being far away, albeit side squalls in the shape of casualty lists, city shops and factories turned to making war materials, and a massive hospital complex had blossomed. Attacking Union armies always had one hand tied behind its back with the nervous federal government fearing for the safety of Washington, DC, while the other was being simultaneously urged to take the Rebel capital at Richmond. Further, it was a long and vulnerable supply line for any Yankee army that attempted to strike deep into the central part of Virginia. So Lynchburg had been spared the wreckage of combat. But by mid-June 1864 the situation had changed, the "Hill City" was being threatened.

Gen. David Hunter, with a force of over 8,000, began his drive in late May. At a place called Piedmont, about ten miles north of Staunton, on June 5th, he thrashed, shattered and scattered a much smaller Confederate army under an out-maneuvered commander named Gen. William E. "Grumble" Jones, who lost his life in the process. The next day Hunter occupied Staunton. Here he was re-inforced by 10,000 additional troops, brought in from the western part of the state. On June 9th Hunter, now with a strength of 18,000, including six artillery batteries with thirty-four guns, with all but four being rifled pieces, issued his orders for the next phase. His army would move up the Valley in four columns, each column composed of either an infantry or cavalry division. The infantry divisions of Genls. Jeremiah Sullivan and George Crook and the cavalry division of William Averell, would move by parallel roads up the Valley. Gen. Alfred Duffié and his cavalry division would pass along the western face of the Blue Ridge Mountains, sending raiding parties to the east side when opportunities were presented. Hunter made his headquarters with Sullivan.[13]

But it is hard to understand how the Union high command really expected much from this force, led as it was by a collection of second raters. For the North, such mediocre leadership would continue until the arrival of General Sheridan. For the South, its commanders there would continue to be better than their opponents, though a second Stonewall Jackson was not to be found waiting.

In Gen. David Hunter, West Point class of 1822, the North possessed more of a vindictive, ultra-rabid abolitionist politician-crusader than a military commander. The reasons for his selection are now lost in time. But as a replacement for Sigel had obviously been needed, Grant, newly installed as commander of all the Federal armies, was not altogether familiar with faces in the eastern theater. Its generals were largely unknown quantities to him. Grant was also reluctant to give up one of the better generals in Meade's army, since a major campaign by this force was already underway. So he apparently deferred the selection to Secretary of War Stanton. Hunter was casually known to Grant but he was better known to President Lincoln and to Stanton, having made the inaugural journey with him to Washington, DC, in 1861.

David Hunter had resigned from the Army in 1836, then returned for Mexican War service. In 1861 he was appointed a colonel of cavalry and had been severely wounded at First Bull Run. After recovering from his wound, Hunter had served the next three years in a variety of posts in the West and Deep South, quickly displaying his fierce abolitionist views by prematurely liberating slaves, which the government in Washington instantly repudiated. So the reason for Hunter's selection was that Grant was too busy to become intimately involved with an appointment where it was obvious that his superiors knew the candidate better than he. There was also probably a reluctance to take anyone from Meade's "First Team" in light of the opposing Confederate command in the Valley being seen as weak. Hunter, who was available, was also an abolitionist, so his appointment might politically placate that segment in the North.[14]

So it was that this man with distant collateral Virginia family roots was chosen to wreak havoc among Virginians. Hunter as a commander would not survive long after the Lynchburg Campaign, replaced by Grant's choice this time, Gen. Philip H. Sheridan. After blaming everyone else for his failure at Lynchburg, Hunter would have one last shot at fame, or infamy, depending on one's point of view, when he headed the "trial" of the Lincoln conspirators. But the record of his campaign in the Valley in 1864 left bitter memories in the minds of Virginians, some lingering to this day, as he burned homes ruthlessly and seemingly without due or proper cause.

As to Hunter's subordinates, Jeremiah Sullivan, commanding one of Hunter's infantry divisions, was a thirty-four-year-old non-professional soldier who had risen from captaincy of an Indiana regiment in 1861. His service prior to Lynchburg had been entirely in the western theater and the Valley armies. He had been a general officer since April 1862, but had no outstanding actions to his credit. He apparently was believed to be dependable but not brilliant. Hunter had no use for him and tried unsuccessfully to have him replaced. Still, he did not perform badly at Piedmont but did not shine at Lynchburg.[15]

General Jeremiah Sullivan
One of Hunter's infantry division commanders, Hunter did not want Sullivan and tried unsuccessfully to have him replaced. He had an undistinguished record with the Federal western armies and did not add to it at Lynchburg.

Hunter's other infantry division commander was George Crook, an 1852 graduate of West Point. He had begun his service fighting Indians and then, like Sullivan, had served in the western theater and the Valley. His general's commission was dated September 1862. A quiet, pleasant-looking fellow, his service seems to have been spotty or erratic, sometimes dull and unimaginative and at other times aggressive. In the early 1864 service in the western part of Virginia, his service was seen by Col. Rutherford B. Hayes, eventually to become president of the United States, as "the best general I have ever known." At Lynchburg he would not stand out as particularly brilliant. But surprisingly, he would later rise to the command of the cavalry of the Army of the Potomac, and then, following the Civil War, serve as a senior commander in the Indian fighting army once again. His service there would be less than stellar; in the Custer Campaign of 1876 he was less than outstanding. In his later years he would quarrel with all of his superiors over battlefield tactics, even breaking with his old friend Philip Sheridan. Crook contended in his memoirs that throughout his entire military career, he had been surrounded with military incompetents![16]

William Averell, commanding one of the two cavalry divisions, had a checkered career as a cavalry commander. A graduate of West Point in 1855, Averell had a variety of cavalry commands. Once Hooker's cavalry chief, he clashed with him and was relieved. His commission also dated from September 1862. At Lynchburg he seems

General George Crook
The second of Hunter's two infantry division commanders, Crook was probably the best of the less than outstanding group. He would later acquire fame as an Indian fighter but did not perform well during the fatal Custer Campaign of 1876.

General William W. Averell
Commander of one of Hunter's two cavalry divisions, Averell was a man with a strange paradox —he showed aggressiveness at Lynchburg, although earlier he had been relieved by Hooker and was later relieved by Sheridan for lack of aggressiveness.

to have been the more aggressive of Hunter's commanders but later, in September 1864, he was relieved of command by Gen. Sheridan for lack of aggressiveness.[17]

In command of Hunter's other cavalry division was Alfred Duffié, a French soldier of fortune who had falsely represented himself to President Lincoln as a former senior French veteran officer and graduate of the French military school of St. Cyr, when in fact he was an errant enlisted man from that army. But in one of the odd miracles of military careering, Duffié, who never displayed much command skill, and even in this campaign would prove inept, was given a colonel's rank, and then achieved a general's star that he retained until the war's end. In the Lynchburg Campaign, Duffié seems to have incurred both Hunter's and Averell's wrath early on, and in the actions directly in front of Lynchburg his accomplishments as given in his after-action report are highly suspect.[18]

General Alfred Duffié
Commander of Hunter's left wing cavalry division, Duffié was not the veteran French military officer he pretended to be and performed poorly for Hunter.

Commanding Hunter's artillery was a young captain named Henry A. DuPont, another West Point graduate, class of 1861. He seems to have been one of the few outstanding officers in Hunter's command. By an odd quirk, DuPont had applied for admission to the Virginia Military Institute (VMI), but was denied on the basis that he was not a resident of the Commonwealth, a requirement at that time. He then went to West Point and became the Chief of Artillery to Hunter, commanding his own regular army battery and three volunteer batteries. At Lexington he apparently deliberately did only some token shelling

Colonel Henry A. DuPont
Hunter's chief of artillery, DuPont was a young captain of the class of 1861 from West Point. Probably the best commander in Hunter's army, he would later become a U.S. senator from Delaware. Photo courtesy Hagley Museum and Library.

of the VMI barracks and had disapproved of Hunter's torching of the school. He along with several other officers of Hunter's command would thoroughly disapprove of Hunter's conduct toward civilians and their property in the campaign. He was the main proponent in later years, as a U.S. senator from Delaware, to enact a $100,000 indemnity to VMI for that damage. That money was used to build the Jackson Memorial Hall. Earlier, at New Market, Colonel DuPont had ably covered Sigel's retreat, and performed well at Piedmont with his massing of guns; at Lynchburg, DuPont would prove himself to be a most able artillery commander and determined proponent of massing guns.[19]

Such was the combined Federal force, a fairly powerful reaper from which much rich grain was expected but little would be harvested. Hunter, after plundering Staunton and wasting a day, started with his main force from that place on June 10th, toward the Valley town of Lexington. After burning the VMI barracks and sacking much of the town, further delaying him, he moved southwestward toward Buchanan on the James River. There he crossed the James and swung east through a pass at Peaks of Otter down to the village of Liberty, present day Bedford. Lynchburg, believed to be weakly held, as was the case, would then be only a two-day march.

Also on June 10th Duffié's command left for its mission to skirt the western slopes of the Blue Ridge Mountains, sending raiding parties through the passes in the mountains to the east side into Nelson and Amherst counties. There his men cut the Orange and Alexandria railroad between Charlottesville and Lynchburg. Duffié then was to cross the James below Lynchburg and tear up the Virginia and Tennessee Railroad along with the canal system. His actions in this move were less than outstanding with his troopers making a few inconsequential raids before being recalled to the main army. There had been a big opportunity to instill panic throughout Lynchburg as a party of his men burned the depot of the critical Orange and Alexandria Railroad at Arrington, east of the Blue Ridge, on the track between Charlottesville and Lynchburg, about twenty-five miles above the city. Then Duffié's small force headed south to the Tye River, six miles north of Amherst courthouse, and the vital railroad bridge spanning it. But here they were rebuffed by a body of some 100 artillerymen of the Botetourt Artillery, turned infantry for a few hours. This unit was on its way northward by train when its commander, Capt. H. C. Douthat, learned of the approach of the raiders. If the raiders destroyed the bridge, the lifeline of Lynchburg northward would be severed, thus delaying Early's timely arrival.

Stopping the northbound train short of the bridge, Douthat unloaded his men, armed them from a supply of muskets stored in a car of the train, and then led the little company across the river to the far side. There in the darkness, Duffié's little raiding party encountered some of Douthat's pickets who fired on them. It appeared that they were men armed with rifles, not cavalry carbines, so the bluecoat troopers assumed they had run into a heavy infantry force and retreated. Then came Hunter's recall that ordered Duffié to withdraw across the mountains to rejoin the main columns.[20] Quick thinking and good leadership on the part of the Confederate junior officer had thus played a major role in saving the city. Had the Tye River bridge been destroyed, Early's Corps would never have reached Lynchburg in time to save it. Several days later, Averell, disgusted with Duffié, dispatched a second party of some 100 troopers under a mere lieutenant on another raid to cut the rail and canal communications east of Lynchburg. This force did little damage before rejoining the main army when it reached Liberty on June 15th.

Grant wanted to starve out his adversary in Petersburg by rendering the Shenandoah Valley of Virginia a wasteland and to destroy railheads at Lynchburg and Charlottesville. The Virginia Central RR from the Valley and the Southside RR from Lynchburg were allowing Lee to stubbornly protect the Confederate capital. To that end, Grant wrote to Hunter that Maj. General Philip Sheridan with his 6,000 man cavalry would destroy the Virginia Central RR and then proceed to Charlottesville to join their forces. The combined army would descend to the Hill City along what is now Rt. 29, destroying the Orange and Alexandria RR.

However, two important circumstances prevented that strategy. First, Hunter did not receive Grant's message and so he proceeded to take the alternate approach route to Lynchburg from the west, and Confederate Gen. Wade Hampton was detached by Lee to intercept the Union menace. With 5,000 mounted troops, Hampton clashed with Sheridan on June 11 just north of a railroad depot called Trevillian's Station, a few miles northeast of Charlottesville. Both cavalries dismounted and fought in dense underbrush and trees. Sheridan's first division was thwarted so he sent in a second division, smashing Hampton's front. As the graycoats retreated, they then met Brig. George A. Custer who had earlier surprised Hampton's wagon trains and horses. Hampton's troopers charged and a furious struggle ensued with Custer's beleaguered cavalry barely escaping. Both sides then retired and prepared for the next day's battle.

When Sheridan's horsemen attacked the Virginia Central RR the next morning of June 12th, a stunning Confederate counterattack that afternoon broke the entire Union line. Darkness ended the day's battle and at dawn the next day the Federals backtracked toward Cold Harbor, burdened with their wounded and runaway slaves.

The combination of the Confederate victory at Trevillian's Station and the fouled message to General Hunter had important implications for the survival of Lynchburg. Had Sheridan not been thwarted and had Grant's message reached Hunter in time to combine their forces, they would have descended from Charlottesville to Lynchburg, destroying the Orange and Alexandria RR along the way. Since that eventuality was avoided, General Jubal Early was allowed open access to ride the rails to the Hill City on June 16-18 to save the city.

The Confederate command in the city had foreseen the initial threat as coming from the north so the commander of the city, Gen. Francis T. Nicholls, a veteran of Lee's Army of Northern Virginia, who had lost an arm and a leg fighting with Lee, formed a corps of 1,000 or more hospital inmates recovering from illnesses and injuries to begin digging fortifications across the James River, atop Amherst Heights. Douthat's battery was also on hand, and for a time, went into position there. But all Nicholls had to man these fortifications were the local militia and "walking wounded" from the hospitals, until help arrived. These same men manned these works on the 16th and 17th but were moved the next day to the new line Early established that guarded approaches to Lynchburg from the west. A determined raid by Duffié's men, if they had chased off Douthat's men at the Tye River, might have brushed aside this weak defense and destroyed or badly damaged the critical bridge over the James into the city proper. Lynchburg would have been isolated.

CHAPTER 4

Hunter Leaves a Terrible Legacy

Following Breckinridge's Confederate victory at New Market on May 15th a period of confidence emerged that the Valley was safe for the time being. Breckinridge and his division had been sent to join Lee's main army facing Grant and Meade. But then came the defeat at Piedmont June 5th. The army there had been thoroughly shattered and Hunter, with some 18,000 men, was on the loose. The supply center of Staunton had been seized and sacked, accompanied by excessive looting. Lee had to take desperate measures.

His first step was to return Breckinridge and his small 2-brigade 2,000-man division to Rockfish Gap. Here he would watch Hunter's moves and deny him the use of that pass, thus protecting Lynchburg from a northern advance. McCausland, alone with some 1,500-2,000 mounted men, was left to deter Hunter's advance up the Valley toward Buchanan and the crossing over the mountains there toward Lynchburg. Another cavalry command under Gen. John Imboden guarded other passes from the Valley into the counties of Nelson and Amherst north of Lynchburg, as well as the critical Orange and Alexandria Railroad that led to Lynchburg from points in the central part of Virginia.

On June 11th, some thirty-five miles south of Staunton, Hunter reached the North River, now the Maury, on the east edge of the Valley village of Lexington. Facing him there was the very small force of a few thousand cavalry and a battery of cannon led by Gen. John McCausland. The general later described his command as really being "mounted infantry" rather than cavalry. But it was never McCausland's intent to stop Hunter there. Not having the manpower, all he could do was delay him in hopes that reinforcements could be found to repel him at a later time.

Hunter quickly drove the southerners back from the heights above the river, then apparently threw a pontoon bridge over it and by this and the remains of the partially Confederate-burned wooden bridge, crossed and entered the village. He then continued more of the ruthless and unwarranted acts he had begun days earlier—acts that were outside the rules of war and are still recalled in some quarters with horror and disgust. He previously hanged a civilian without trial for shooting a drunken soldier who had intruded the man's home and molested his wife.

After shelling and burning the barracks at VMI, a perfectly legal military action, he then proceeded to destroy countless non-military items at VMI and the adjacent Washington College, now known as Washington and Lee University. Libraries, teaching equipment, scientific instruments and collections, texts, and other non-military properties were destroyed. The home of former Governor John Letcher was burned on a flimsy pretext along with several other homes. Additionally, Hunter's men looted the Lexington citizenry —unwarranted acts against civilians and their property. Word of Hunter's viciousness quickly spread as he moved farther up the Valley, giving Hunter the nickname "Hunter, the Hyena."

But in Lexington he made a tactical blunder. He paused, contending that he needed to allow a 200-wagon supply train en route to him from Staunton to catch up with him. It was a significant delay. For two more days he lingered in Lexington; he had already lost time by not moving quickly from Staunton. It would be the 14th before

The VMI barracks following Hunter's raid. Courtesy VMI Archives.

he resumed his march. But while in Lexington, Hunter learned that Lee was apparently shifting some sort of force over to augment the Confederate troops defending the Valley. The type and strength was unknown.

Meanwhile, the Confederate command in Lynchburg quickly learned of Hunter's approach as he left Lexington on June 14th and headed up the valley to Buchanan, on the west side of the Blue Ridge from Lynchburg. In the city, rumors abounded, and by June 15th the telegraph wires hummed between General Nicholls, the commanding officer at Lynchburg, Superintendent Gen. F. H. Smith, whose cadets had fled Lexington and were then guarding the pass near Glasgow, and Genls. Imboden and McCausland, as they tried to update each other regarding Hunter's whereabouts and progress.

General John C. Breckinridge
A good politician turned excellent soldier, Breckinridge was the winner at New Market. He preceded Early in command at Lynchburg. Injuries relegated him to a lesser role in fighting. He would shortly become the Confederate Secretary of War.

Late on June 14th it was obvious Hunter was aiming at Lynchburg. To the north of Lynchburg, at Rockfish Gap, was General Breckinridge, a former United States Vice President and excellent politician now turned excellent general. Breckinridge was a rarity in that he made for a very competent military commander. Having been sent by Lee to reinforce the Confederate strength in the Valley, he took up a blocking position there. But when he learned of Hunter's move up the Valley he was astute enough to see that his position there had become useless. He then moved his thin infantry division to Lynchburg, arriving with part of his men on the 15th and the rest arriving on June 16th. Upon arriving he immediately took over command from Nicholls, but not for long. Breckinridge was in poor physical shape also; his horse had fallen upon him a few weeks earlier and injured him badly. He was now in great pain, running a fever and suffering from chronic diarrhea. Dr. E. A. Craighill, who attended the general, found him to be "entirely unfit for service." Therefore, at 5:30 p.m. on June 16th, he turned over command to his senior brigade commander, Gen. John C. Vaughn, advising him that Early was to arrive the next day, and until then Vaughn was to coordinate with Gen. Daniel H. Hill, who was in the city. Also offering his services was veteran commander, Gen. Harry Hays, who was in the hospital in Lynchburg recovering from a wound.[21]

It remained to be seen, however, whether double-amputee Gen. Francis Nicholls, injured General Hays, Breckinridge's weak infantry command, some 250 cadets, and a handful of boys, old men and crippled soldiers, with an *ad hoc* commander would be able to stave off capture until help arrived. Fortunately for the Confederacy, Lee was fully aware of the impending danger to his vital supply base and gave orders on June 12th for General Early to move quickly with the II Corps—some 8,000 men and twenty-four guns, to the defense of Lynchburg. But it was a desperate race against time.

General Francis Nicholls
A West Point 1855 graduate, Nicholls had been severely wounded twice while fighting against Lee. He was in command at Lynchburg until Early's arrival.

While Nicholls had just a small number of militia, about 600 according to one account, plus 1,300 "walking wounded," he had no regular troops initially to defend Lynchburg. However, by June 15th, there were three small, regular commands heading toward the city to augment its meager defenses. Breckinridge's 2,000-man infantry division began entering the city on the 16th. Also moving toward the city were the two cavalry commands of Genls. John C. Imboden and John C. McCausland, veterans of Valley fighting. Both commands numbered probably less than 2,000 men each, and both men and horses were jaded.

Another small force also soon arrived. These were the 250 cadets from VMI who had been blocking a pass near present-day Glasgow on the James River, seventeen miles south of Lexington. When Breckinridge learned Hunter was headed toward Buchanan, he ordered the cadets to cross the mountains to Snowden and there take canal boats down the James River to Lynchburg. Upon their arrival on the 16th, they were put to work digging trenches and a redoubt on the west edge of the city, guarding the road from Lynchburg to Lexington. The site of a redoubt they probably built stood on the rise now occupied by a mansion called Villa Maria on Rivermont Avenue. As late as 1939, VMI historian Col. William Cooper reported in his work *One Hundred Years at V.M.I.* that the trenches dug by the cadets were still visible in the fields between Spring Street and Victoria Avenue. But today no readily visible trenches remain. Everyone in the Confederate command in the city, to say nothing of the citizenry, waited and watched the railroad tracks that led northward. All knew by now that General Early and his II Corps were coming. Would they make it in time?

Section of inner defense line trenches, probably dug by VMI cadets. Photo taken in the Old City Cemetery.

CHAPTER 5

The Confederate Generals — No Pushovers

When Hunter left Lexington on June 14th, McCausland kept his command in Hunter's front, harassing and delaying him. Imboden's troopers, who had been following Duffié, still guarded the passes in the area just west of the Blue Ridge and tried to deter his efforts to sever the rail line between Charlottesville and Lynchburg. At Rockfish Gap, Breckinridge, upon learning of Hunter's direction, turned his troops about and marched toward Lynchburg. When Duffié rejoined Hunter's main column, Imboden moved his cavalry over the mountains to reinforce Lynchburg, arriving in the city on June 16th. He was immediately sent for by Breckinridge to reinforce McCausland, still in front of Hunter and delaying him as best he could. Could the city be held until reinforcements from Lee arrived?

At this point in time, if the Federal command was a mixed bag of less than outstanding commanders, the Confederate command in Lynchburg was also badly muddled. Nicholls had been the local commander in the city, but when Breckinridge arrived Nicholls turned over command to him. Breckinridge was still suffering badly from the injury earlier of his horse falling on him. He accordingly turned over command to his senior infantry commander Gen. John C. Vaughn. However, veteran General Daniel H. Hill, then

General Daniel H. Hill

General Harry T. Hays

without a command, had made his way to the city to see if he could help. Additionally, Gen. Harry T. Hays, another veteran combat commander, was in the city at the huge military hospital recovering from a wound, and he, too, offered his services. It was probably in the morning of the 16th that Breckinridge directed Vaughn to take over but coordinate his actions with Hill.

By early afternoon Vaughn proved lacking, quite dilatory in Breckinridge's view, and Breckinridge promptly wired Richmond for a replacement.[22] He had also become dissatisfied, for unspecified reasons, with Imboden's conduct and asked for a replacement for him as well. Imboden did not have a lofty reputation with some of his commanders who often viewed him as lax in discipline and tending to act too independently. However, his actions in front of Hunter on June 17th - 18th seem to have been satisfactory enough.

Richmond headquarters also responded quickly, sending Gen. Arnold Elzey, a West Pointer and former brigade commander under Jackson to take over Vaughn's command. To replace Imboden, Gen. Robert Ransom was sent, another West Pointer and veteran brigade commander from Lee's army. Early, in his 1866 account, infers that both men arrived sometime on the after-

General Arnold Elzey
A veteran combat commander, Elzey had not had much field service since being badly wounded in 1862. He was called in from Richmond to replace Breckinridge as division commander and probably commanded Early's left on June 18 and 19.

noon of the 18th. However, it was not until Early arrived in person on June 17th that a single healthy man carrying the reputation of a hard battling commander took total and complete charge of the forces in Lynchburg.

While Early was moving his troops toward Charlottesville, Hunter had been steadily moving. At Buchanan he again scattered a force of McCausland's men, though they had managed to burn the bridge over the James River there. McCausland himself barely escaped capture when he fell from the bridge as it was being set afire. Swimming around for a few seconds, he spotted a nearby skiff and climbed aboard. Paddling his way across to the south side, he made his escape. Thus Hunter was delayed yet another day as his engineers rebuilt the span.[23]

The next day Hunter resumed his march, though the ever-annoying McCausland was still active, blowing up parts of the main road through the mountains and felling trees as further hindrance, forcing Hunter's column to deploy. Hunter was forced to use a secondary road two miles south of Buchanan, a very steep and winding passage

Moving from the Shenandoah Valley across the Blue Ridge Mountains, Hunter's army passed through the gap between the Peaks of Otter, about 45 miles southwest of Lynchburg.

over the mountains.[24] The column moved slowly. Hunter's horses were tired and worn, having been in constant use since late May. The army was now reduced in part to living off the land, land that his quartermaster said was less bountiful than the lower Valley they had previously traversed. When they had reached Buchanan they were already short of hardtack and flour, though they still had adequate supplies of beef and mutton. Finally, by nightfall of June 15, the tired harassed army went into camp near the small city then called Liberty, now known as Bedford. The next day he would move on Lynchburg. Hunter was told that the city of Lynchburg was poorly defended and ready to be seized. There seemed no reason to rush.

Interesting is an entry in the diary of Col. William Tibbitts, the commanding officer of the 21st New York Calvary Regiment of Duffié's division for June 16th. About the time the Federal column made its turn onto the secondary road over the mountains south, Tibbitts noted that Hunter continued his willful practice of burning civilian homes. This time it was the fine structure owned by Col. J. T. Anderson called "Mount Joy." The home contained a wonderful library, was rich in antiques, and filled with works of art. Anderson was the younger brother of Gen. Joseph R. Anderson who commanded the Tredegar Iron Works in Richmond, a major source of arms for the Confederacy. This was grounds enough for Hunter. "Burn it!" came the order from Hunter to a lieutenant of Tibbitts' command! The officer was appalled. With that Hunter left and moved on. The lieutenant decided to weaken the order by burning only the outbuildings.[25]

A short while later Hunter learned that his full order had not been obeyed and called the young officer before him. In a bad mood and temper, Hunter reprimanded him and directed that he return forthwith and carry out the order. The reluctant lieutenant returned and woefully carried out the order but not before giving the family a full hour to save what they could before he set it on fire. If one was to characterize the regimental commanders of both armies North and South, the word "gentlemen" would no doubt be a common description; they waged war to their utmost but by and large, refrained from committing needless outrages on the civilian community. Thus Tibbitts' entry seems evidence that yet another of

Hunter's officers did not subscribe to their commander's pyromaniac tendencies.

While the Federal high command of the Union attacking force was certainly of less than outstanding caliber, the Confederate commanders were also a mixed bag, but of generally better quality. As the battle seemed to be nearing, the question of overall Confederate commander was settled—Jubal Early. He was a man of extreme contrasts; he could be unbelievably kind and polite, and then be incredibly rude, caustic and quarrelsome. He had few friends and cared less. An 1837 West Point Military Academy graduate, he had resigned from the army after a year of service. He then took up law and politics, though he returned to service during the Mexican War. Initially an opponent of secession, he joined his state's military forces and fought in a distinguished manner at First Manassas. This won him his first general officer's star.

From 1861 through 1863 Early had proved to be an able brigade commander, a tough, aggressive division commander, and for a time satisfactory Corps commander, filling in for the wounded Gen. Richard Ewell. On May 29th, just weeks before his move to Lynchburg, Early had been promoted to permanent command of the II Corps. Early was also noted to not only be foul of tongue at times but to be ever ready to tangle with the Yankees. He carried with him at all times a particularly deep disgust for the combat capabilities of cavalry—no matter whose it was. There would come a day when he would learn its true usefulness.

While there are some who have questioned Early's ability to serve as a Corps commander, the eminent Confederate historian Dr. Douglas Southall Freeman said of Early that "his fighting record from Cedar Mountain to Salem Church stands second only to that of Jackson himself." In 1864, Jubal Early was the right man at the right place. Hunter, as time would shortly reveal at Cedar Creek, may have been a classic example of the "Peter Principle" in that he had been promoted one grade above what he was truly capable of handling. Lynchburg, however, was the highlight of his military career.

Under Early were several general officers of mixed capabilities. John C. Breckinridge was an able politician turned excellent soldier. He has a record of being a satisfactory division commander in the West and Deep South and certainly handled his force well at New Market where he had been the commander. He had not had the chance to show his full worth as a division commander under Lee as his service with the Army of Northern Virginia had been extremely short. But now he had already shown some battlefield savvy by the prompt move of his division from Rockfish Gap to Lynchburg. Some writers have placed him in charge of the Confederate's rightwing; however, his bad physical condition would seem to indicate otherwise. Also, it appears that Elzey arrived in time to take over this flank for the afternoon of June 18th. In February of 1865 Breckinridge would give up his sword to become President Jefferson Davis's last Secretary of War.

Calvary commander John C. McCausland, whose delaying tactics against Hunter were effective, was an 1857 graduate of VMI, graduating first in his class. His war service up to this time had been in the West as a brigade commander. On May 18, 1864, he was promoted to a general officer rank and given command of a cavalry brigade opposing Hunter. He executed well his delaying tactic role subsequent to the Confederate defeat at Piedmont. Hunter's move up the Valley from Lexington found McCausland always in his front, sniping, cutting trees to bar roads, burning bridges, and constantly slowing the Union advance. When the war ended he refused to surrender at Appomattox, escaping to Europe and Mexico for several years before finally returning to his farm in West Virginia.[26]

General John C. McCausland
A master at delaying tactics, McCausland annoyed Hunter greatly for the entire campaign. The citizens of Lynchburg honored him for his services in saving the city. Photo courtesy West Virginia State Archives.

The other senior Confederate cavalry commander present, John D. Imboden, was a lawyer and legislator turned soldier. He had begun his service as an artilleryman but soon moved to the command of a partisan ranger battalion, and was promoted to general officer rank in October 1862. During Lee's Gettysburg Campaign, Imboden had covered the army's left flank and masked its retreat, but there is evidence Lee was less than pleased with Imboden's performance during the campaign. His partisan background and apparent lack of discipline with his men had not set well with some of his commanders. In the Lynchburg Campaign he seems to have carried out a delaying role somewhat independently although well. But he was replaced sometime on the 18th by General Ransom and would never again hold an active military command.

General John D. Imboden
Imboden performed well at Lynchburg but had previously incurred displeasure with some of the Confederate high command. Illness forced his retirement from field command shortly after the Lynchburg battle.

Also under Early's immediate command were three division commanders who had been proven in battle—Stephen D. Ramseur, John B. Gordon, and Robert E. Rodes. Ramseur, a West Pointer, class of 1860, was a true combat veteran of Lee's army. Ambitious and fearless, he was nursing a mangled right arm from a wound suffered in the vicious fighting at Malvern Hill. In the infantry fighting that

General Stephen D. Ramseur
A veteran combat commander under Early and recently elevated to division commander, Ramseur and his division led Early's Corps into Lynchburg on June 17th and saw the heaviest action. Photo courtesy N.C. Office of Archives and History.

would ensue in front of Lynchburg, Ramseur and his men would see the heaviest action. Four months later at Winchester, Ramseur fell, mortally wounded. He learned of the birth of his daughter just hours before he died. When he expired his West Point friends of an earlier day: George A. Custer, Henry A. DuPont and Wesley Merritt were present.

General Robert E. Rodes
A native Lynchburger and aggressive combat commander, Rodes led a division under Early which probably did not reach the field until the fighting on the 18th was over. He was killed at Winchester in September 1864.

Similarly, Lynchburger Robert E. Rodes, VMI class of 1848, teacher and engineer before turning soldier, was also killed three months later at Winchester. He, too, was a fighter and combat veteran, wounded at Fair Oaks and again at Sharpsburg. In the emergency following Jackson's wounding at Chancellorsville, Rodes succeeded to the command of the Corps until "Jeb" Stuart took over. Early had no reason to doubt Rodes' ability; certainly Lee had expressed great confidence in him. While Rodes and his men would not reach the Lynchburg battle area until after Hunter had begun his retreat, Rodes' strong command was nice to have in reserve.[27]

General John B. Gordon
A fiery, capable division commander under Early, part of Gordon's division may have been in action on June 17th and all of the division on June 18th.

John B. Gordon had been a lawyer and coal mine superintendent before becoming an infantry colonel of the 6th Alabama infantry regiment in the Army of Northern Virginia. Gordon received a promotion to general officer level in November 1862, following outstanding service at Sharpsburg where he had been wounded. He became a mainstay in Lee's army, enjoying the reputation of being a scrapper. After the short stay in the Valley with Early, he returned to Lee's main army and fought with it until Appomattox. He was a first class commander in whom Early could place complete trust.[28]

Brigade commanders under Breckinridge were Gen. John A. Wharton and Col. George S. Patton. Both Wharton and Patton were VMI graduates and both had performed well at New Market. Wharton was known to be a stubborn fighter, but allegedly President Davis did not like him and never moved him from the western area of Virginia to a more prominent command position in Lee's army. There is also some question as to whether Wharton was on the field these two days, as Col. Augustus Forsberg may have commanded the brigade on June 17 and 18.[29]

Patton was in the mold of his grandson Gen. "Georgie" S. Patton of WWII days. But oddly enough, Mark Boatner in his fine work *The Civil War Dictionary* makes no mention of either men, albeit the book is an excellent short compendium of biographies, events and actions. Overall, the Lynchburg Campaign possessed a Confederate leadership that was more able than their Union counterparts.

CHAPTER 6

Smoke on the Horizon

During the night of June 16 and 17 Hunter set up camp around the village of Liberty. Several of Hunter's officers were not happy with his earlier burning of a number of houses and there can be little doubt that he became aware of this. In Liberty he continued the burning of supplies and buildings that could be deemed of military value and tore up some six miles of railroad track and the depot. Later, however, when a civilian was reported to have passed information that the Confederates had inflicted serious damage on Federal armies in both the eastern and western theaters, Hunter became outraged and promptly ordered the house the man was living in burned to the ground.

To his credit, there was no reported misconduct toward the many wounded Confederate soldiers in the various houses and buildings being used as hospital recovery wards. But there were reports of hungry soldiers looting private homes in search of food. Indeed, men of the 116th Ohio Infantry reported that they had been on half-rations for days and were now told there was no more to be had. It is not surprising, then, that there was considerable looting, and some of it no doubt took on more than a search for food. General Crook later commented that Hunter had "kept us at destroying the railway instead of dashing on and into Lynchburg." That night Hunter received information from the interrogation of the wife of a Confederate soldier who had just returned to Liberty from Lynchburg that the city was not well fortified. This was true enough at that moment so Hunter delayed and failed to push. The next morning would be time enough.

Hunter was up about 2:00 a.m. on the 17th. His men broke camp at dawn as Hunter wanted an early start. His columns headed out by several roads toward Lynchburg, twenty-five miles distant. Moving on Hunter's far left, on a road called the Old Forest Road, was the cavalry division of General Duffié. General Averell's cavalry division was positioned on the Federal right, leading the way, just off to the right of the main road, the Salem-Lynchburg Pike, now US 460. Behind them, on the Salem-Lynchburg Pike, came the two infantry divisions. According to Humphreys, Crook's division marched astride the railroad, destroying it as they went. Sullivan's command followed with DuPont's artillery batteries and the army's wagon trains bringing up the rear. These forces intended to drive into the city from the south, but their progress was met with delays, which infuriated Hunter. The bridge over the Big Otter River outside Liberty had been burned by McCausland the day before and Hunter's road-bound army came to a grinding halt! Back went the call for engineers and these began searching about for what they believed were the proper supplies with which to rebuild the span. An hour passed, the troops of the 116th Ohio Infantry waiting nearby watched in disgust. They grew impatient and began cutting logs to rebuild the bridge on their own. An hour later the bridge was repaired and the Union columns began moving again.[30]

Unknown to Hunter at this time was the fact that Early and the lead elements of his Corps were already on their way and would begin arriving in Lynchburg about 1:00 p.m. Breckinridge, who commanded the Lynchburg defenses, had taken some significant steps before his injury forced him to turn over command. His infantry began digging entrenchments on the College Hill site at the city's southern edge. Further, he decided to send Imboden's cavalry out on the Salem-Lynchburg Pike, to reinforce McCausland, whose tired men were still in front of the Federals, stalling their approach. Breckinridge also urged the continued construction of the defensive works at the city's edge that Nicholls had begun as a final defense line. Duffié's approach from the west along the Old Forest Road was initially undetected and unopposed to this point.

But as soon as Duffié's presence astride the Old Forest Road was discovered, Imboden, as the senior officer on the field, ordered McCausland to move his brigade to face Duffié. Imboden also sent at least two guns.[31] There is some evidence that McCausland may also have had a battery, or parts thereof, with him since Lexington.

As Imboden had reported on the night of June 16th that he had with him four rifled guns and two small howitzers, the two guns he sent were probably the lighter more maneuverable howitzers to block the Old Forest Road. There was adequate force then astride the Old Forest Road to delay Duffié. Whether McCausland retained both of Imboden's howitzers along with any of his artillery is unknown. But in light of the very difficult terrain over which he would be fighting, it is likely he sent the heavier artillery to the rear and kept the two lighter pieces. Meanwhile Breckinridge or Hill set Breckinridge's men to work digging on the fortifications along the line Nicholls may have recommended, namely the high ground from College Hill over to the vicinity of the Old Methodist Cemetery. The VMI cadets were put to work digging from the cemetery over to the Lexington Road.

It was about midday when Hunter and his main force finally crossed the Otter River and resumed their march headed toward a hamlet called New London, twelve miles from Lynchburg, This was a tiny village where it was hoped that with the coming of the Virginia and Tennessee Railroad it would develop into the new London of the new world. This hoped for growth, however, failed to materialize. At New London, Averell's troopers were momentarily delayed again by the Confederate cavalry, but they quickly brushed the Rebel force back and resumed the march toward the city of Lynchburg. As this was happening, Early arrived in Lynchburg with the initial detachment of his troops and sought out Breckinridge. It was around 1:00 p.m. when Early wired Richmond that he had arrived with "sufficient troops to make all safe." It was probably a half hour later when Early located Breckinridge. He found him quite ill and bedridden. Gen. D. H. Hill was with him as well. Early formally advised both men that, by order of General Lee, he was assuming command. He then received an update from Breckinridge on the status in the city; this done, he took his leave, climbed on his horse and set out to investigate the situation throughout the city.[32]

As Early rode out to the quickly prepared inner defenses along the high ground of College Hill, his infantry was arriving at the train station and moving out to bolster the line. As yet, none of his artillery had arrived. Early was no stranger to the city and it environs. In May

1861, as a newly commissioned infantry colonel, he had been on this ground for two months organizing, equipping and training several regiments for the Confederacy. He certainly knew the high ground of the College Hill area at the city's edge and saw where initial efforts to build a defense line had begun, but he quickly noticed that if this position were lost it was within cannon range from there into the heart of town. Early, as he looked about, is reported to have snorted in his often-sarcastic way, "Why in hell didn't you put it on Main Street!"

Indeed this was in a sense true, but Hill or one of the others present must have said something to the effect that with the mere handful of troops available at the time the line was laid out, this was all that could be manned. This line is marked today in a number of places by state historical markers. Early probably gave some sort of comment of disgust and announced he was going to move the defenses farther out, and with that the party rode out southward on the Salem Pike in the direction of the city toll gate a little over two miles away.

One of several state historical markers indicating the position of the inner lines of Lynchburg.

As they rode the sound of gunfire in the distance eventually reached them. Averell's division had pushed Imboden's and McCausland's force grudgingly rearward toward a small stone building, then in partial ruins, that had been a Quaker meeting house. This point was about four miles beyond the inner defense line in the city. Both commands had been hindering every yard of the Federal advance though neither seemed to be operating under any joint direction. Unquestionably, the Confederate cavalry was getting very weary; their horses were close to exhaustion, and the men were running low on ammunition. Then word came of Duffié's approach and McCausland's command was ordered over to the Old Forest Road to block him. There Duffié and McCausland collided around 1:30 p.m. McCausland's troopers dismounted and began fighting from covered ground, his cannon spewing fire and forcing the Federals to deploy in the face of unknown strength. The Confederate troops would then quickly hitch up the guns, mount their own horses, and scurry back to the next defensive spot of ground. Duffié, not showing great generalship, concluded he was being blocked by Rebel infantry—no doubt McCausland's "mounted infantry" who were probably armed with rifles that made a crack different from a calvary carbine. Duffié guardedly moved along the narrow and heavily wooded road.[33]

It was about this time that Early had reached a rise overlooking the Lynchburg city tollgate. The spot was about two miles outside the city limits. Here he paused and surveyed the ground in all directions. It was mostly quite open but it was severely broken ground with deep ravines crisscrossing one another. Here and there were small patches of woods. To the far left there was extremely difficult broken ground and a deep creek—Fishing Creek. To the far right there was another steep banked creek—Blackwater Creek. This site appealed to Early as the place to build his forward defense line as both flanks were protected by waterways that would be difficult to ford. He would not try to man the entire line; rather, place good size units at key points, such as possible crossing points mostly along Blackwater Creek or be in position to rush troops to any threatened point. Early followed the old military adage of Frederick the Great, that he who defends everything defends nothing!

With the sound of gunfire ahead, Ramseur's troops hurried forward to the new line and went to work digging rifle pits and trenches. They manned an existing redoubt on the Salem Turnpike to anchor the center and dominate this main road into the city. This earthwork, a rather sizeable one, later to be known as Fort Early, is one of the few remaining relics of the battle for the city. Ramseur's troops manned the line to the left of this strongpoint. Breckinridge's infantry were hurried forward from the College Hill area to cover the right. Two guns under Lt. Carter Berkeley from John H. McClanahan's battery, a unit that had been with Breckinridge, were ordered to unlimber in the redoubt. Similarly, some guns from Maj. Floyd King's artillery battalion were told to fill out the redoubt.

Berkeley was a veteran of the Valley fighting and had acquired some fame as an outstanding artillery officer. With Berkeley in command, the battery had come into Lynchburg by forced marches, crossing the James River by the Ninth Street Bridge, then over the stone arch that spanned the Kanawha Canal—an arch that still stands—and into the city on the evening of the 16th. His arrival was greeted with immediate urgings to hurry to the front. Hunter was coming! "But where was the front?" asked Berkeley. He was totally ignorant of Lynchburg and its surroundings. Directly ahead, out past the hills, he was told. With that he turned to his men and beckoned them forward. The battery started ahead, diverting to one of the other streets, as Eighth Street at that time did not go directly ahead. All of the streets that led out of Lynchburg to the south were extremely steep. Past the old city market his tired horses pulled the guns and caissons.[34]

Indeed it takes a very hardy soul today to hike non-stop from the foot of Eighth Street to the top. It became obvious that the exhausted teams could not pull the grade alone. Crewmen went beside each wheel and pushed, but even this effort was not enough. At that moment some of Imboden's cavalry were passing at the foot of the hill near Church Street. They saw the trouble, dismounted, and joined with Berkeley's men in pushing the guns, along with the tired teams, to the top. From there they moved as fast as the weary animals could move out to Fort Early where they were eagerly received and ordered into the fort.

On the Confederate far right, Breckinridge's thin brigades moved into positions covering Blackwater Creek and were responsible for the area between Fort Early and another earthwork that covered the ground where Old Forest Road entered the city from the west—the road Duffié was using. This earthwork, which became known as Fort McCausland, also covered a trail that came down from the north off the Lexington Pike and joined Old Forest Road at the bridge over Blackwater Creek. Artillery was placed in the fort—probably about four guns initially. Part of the west face of this fort remains today close by a Jewish Synagogue. Possibly the extreme right infantry unit was Wharton's brigade, now commanded by Col. August Forsberg. Soon

West face of the only remaining portion of Fort McCausland.

two more guns became available for use on that flank and these went into position on high ground just off what is today Clifton Street, to the right rear of Fort McCausland. While these preparations were being made, McCausland's force was still out front covering the extreme right, delaying Duffié.

Until more of his troops arrived, Early's only reserve was apparently just the militia, the walking wounded and the small battalion of VMI cadets. The cadets had come down the James River by canal boats and had reached the city some time on the 16th and put to work digging defenses on the inner line. After they completed their digging, they were ordered into a reserve position behind Fort Early. When more II Corps units arrived the next day the cadets were shifted more to the right to watch the Lexington Road, sleeping that night amid the gravestones of the Old Methodist Cemetery, an event many cadets would later not forget. It was now late afternoon and Early watched and waited, overseeing the construction. But the gunfire in the distance grew closer and more feverish as Hunter's column approached Lynchburg on the Salem Turnpike. Digging his spurs into his horse and making sure his old hat was firmly on his head, the general started at a slow trot toward the firing.

CHAPTER 7

June 17th—A Day of Battle

Regrettably, detailed accounts of individual unit actions for the 17th of June and for the main event the next day are not that numerous nor very revealing. For the Confederate side there is a paucity of contemporary reports and accounts. Most of what is known of their actions must be taken from post-war accounts, many of which may suffer from the usual warping of memory, however unintentional. The limited number of Federal accounts, the lack of clearly definable landmarks in those that are available, total lack of post-war unit markers, and the undulating ground makes unit placement and movement difficult to understand. It seems that the Federal efforts were quite disjointed, due in part to the difficult terrain in which they had to maneuver. Further, there seems to have been a distinct lack of firm command and control. For whatever reason, Hunter's progress was limited and sporadic.

Hunter's force had finally gotten under way again late on the morning of June 17th. As he rode out of Liberty, Hunter left behind a long trail of still smoldering ruins of warehouses, barns, storage buildings, and the depot, which when combined with his unnecessary house burnings, portrayed him in Southern eyes as being no gentleman, even disturbing Col. David Hunter Strother, his kinsman and aide. Duffié's division had moved to the left onto the Old Forest Road that somewhat paralleled the Salem Turnpike but entered Lynchburg from the west. Averell's cavalry division moved to the

Colonel David Hunter Strother
A noted diarist and artist of the campaign.

right off the main Salem Pike, several miles to the right of Crook's and Sullivan's infantry marching on the Pike. The mounted troopers could negotiate broken ground far more readily than the foot soldiers who were better suited to a wider roadway. The distance from the vicinity of Liberty to New London is about fifteen miles, a cavalry travel time of about three to four hours, depending upon conditions.

Averell moved cautiously, knowing the pattern of Confederate delaying tactics, as he later reported, "The enemy resisted our advance at every step...." Averell kept a running stream of messages flowing to Crook, advising him of the cavalry's progress. While Averell's advance was slowed by the Confederate delaying actions, the Union infantry column was delayed for four hours by the rebuilding of the bridge across the Big Otter River.

Col. James M. Schoonmaker's regiments were deployed as skirmishers, as Averell's command moved ahead, with Col. William H. Powell's and Col. John H. Oley's brigades in column to their rear. Suddenly contact was again made with the Confederates. This point approximated the low rise about a half-mile south of the Quaker church. The Federals pushed ahead through wooded and broken ground for a short time. Then resistance stiffened markedly when Averell's troopers came in sight of the ruined stone church, the

Around the ruins of this Quaker meeting house was the initial Confederate defense of the city early on June 17th. Manned by Imboden's cavalry, they were driven from it by the attack of Crook and Sullivan's infantry.

Quaker meeting house, that today stands restored, about four miles out from the old city limits. It was probably just prior to this that the Confederates spotted Duffié's column on the Old Forest Road on the Federal left flank.

To Averell on the right flank it appeared that the enemy had decided to stand and fight yet another harassing and delaying action. He would attack and scatter them once and for all, perhaps even being able to push his way into the city. But the ground was, in Averell's words, "difficult for cavalry" so he changed his formations. One brigade remained mounted with some deployed as skirmishers across open ground. Supporting these he placed other squadrons "with intervals in columns of fours, open order, ready to charge" should the enemy break or dismount and fight on foot. His remaining two brigades were kept in column. The deployment completed, Averell gave the command "Forward!" It was about 4:30 p.m. Confederate commander General Early was at this time in the vicinity of the earthwork, now known as Fort Early, overseeing the construction of the outer defense line there.[35]

Imboden's initial defense position was on a rise a bit in advance of a ridge on which stood the ruined remains of the stone Quaker church. A low, wide valley was to its immediate front. Backing up his troopers was some artillery on the Quaker church ridge. At least one of these guns was a 20-pounder Parrott rifle. Years later a shell for this type gun was discovered under the flooring of the rebuilt church and is now in the Lynchburg City Museum. Weeks earlier, Imboden had reported that he had such a gun along with a big 24-pounder howitzer.

The Federal lines pressed forward and were instantly met by what Averell recalled as small arms fire punctuated by rapid artillery fire. Instantly, Averell's two rearward reserve brigades dismounted and moved up into action. Imboden's men slowly fell back to the high ground around the church ruins, taking cover behind the walls of the meeting house and adjoining cemetery. But to Averell it became apparent that his cavalry was not going to dislodge the enemy line. He also sensed they were setting a trap for him; Averell called a halt and screamed for infantry. To counter the annoying Rebel cannon, he brought forward a section of his own artillery and a noisy gun duel

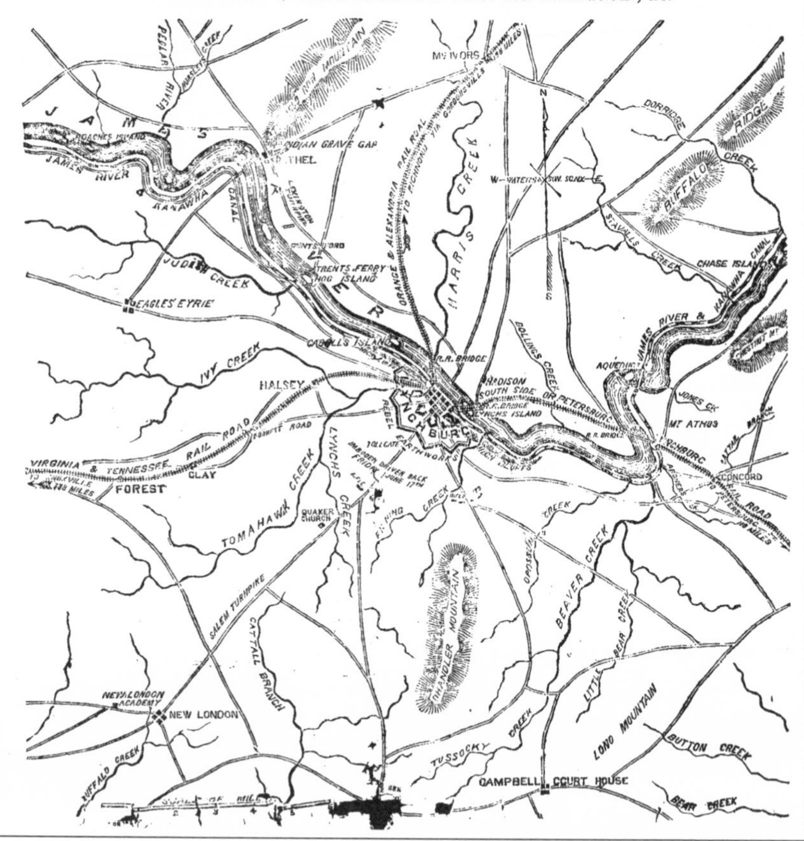

NEW YORK HERALD, MONDAY, JUNE 27, 1864.

LYNCHBURG AND ITS SURROUNDINGS.

Scene of Recent Operations of the Columns Under the Immediate Command of Generals Hunter, Crook and Averill---The Railroad and Water Communications, &c.

Lynchburg Battle map published in a northern newspaper.

ensued. Rebel artillery and musket fire bit into the Federal troops, holding them at bay.

Suddenly some of the Confederate units swarmed out of their cover of stone walls and fence rails and advanced toward the Union troopers. It appeared to the Federals that the enemy was launching a full-scale attack. Averell began looking over his shoulder for the requested infantry as his troops held on. It was nearly dusk. Then, according to Averell, the long blue ranks of Crook's infantry arrived on the field. Anxiously, the blue cavalrymen watched as their infantry columns pealed off into line of battle astride the Turnpike. The first line was composed of the 91st Ohio on the left of one brigade, with its left flank on the Pike and the 12th Ohio on its right. Directly behind came the 14th West Virginia and the 9th West Virginia, the latter with its left on the Pike behind the 91st Ohio. This was the command of Col. Carr B. White. The deployment of the second brigade, that of Col. J. M. Campbell, was on the west side of the Pike. The units halted briefly, dressed ranks, and began to advance through Averell's stalled cavalry.

The Federal line of march took them initially through a patch of heavy woods that concealed deployed Confederate snipers. The Union skirmishers returned fire and drove the Confederates slowly rearward toward their main position among the church ruins. The fighting then emerged into open ground and on into a deep ravine. The Confederate position at the Quaker Church was atop the far edge of that ravine and from there the Rebels poured fire down onto their advancing Federals. The 91st Ohio still had its left flank on the road and was struggling forward when suddenly its commander, Col. J. A. Turley, fell badly wounded; the Lt. Col. B. F. Coates, took over and kept the unit moving forward.

The Ohioans fought through the ravine, and while peering through the battle smoke, they could faintly see to their front the church ruins and the line of rifle pits and rail breastworks. Another quarter mile and they came face to face with the Rebel positions. With a loud yell, the 91st charged, swarming over the defenses, scattering the defenders and capturing two guns, one of which was reported as being a fine English piece, probably a Blakeley. The 91st began to move still farther ahead into another ravine. But then Lt. Col. Coates looked about and to his dismay discovered his regiment was all alone, its sister regiments were nowhere to be seen. Soon darkness would engulf the field, so Coates halted the regiment where it stood. To advance further seemed too risky. Apparently each of the other regiments elsewhere on the field had unilaterally reached the same decision.

As darkness settled in, the Federal units took stock. Casualties in the 91st reflected one officer and eight men killed and three officers including its colonel and nineteen men wounded. The 12th Ohio suffered seven killed and nine wounded. The 14th West Virginia did not report any casualties but sorrowfully reported that one of its officers, a lieutenant, had displayed outright cowardice by running rearward and hiding behind rocks. Across the Turnpike the 15th West Virginia reported two wounded, but reports from the other units were never recorded. Crook contended he had captured some seventy men and one gun. Thus, neither Hunter's infantry nor his cavalry had suffered grievous losses to their fighting power. But now a new bit of fresh intelligence began to emerge and filter rearward. Confederate prisoners boasted that Early's famed II Corps was either on the field in part or soon to be present in its entirety.[36] Hunter now had to face up to the possibility that he apparently no longer was facing just a relatively small cavalry force. If this was the case, then a very sour quince had been tossed into Hunter's heretofore sweet and as yet unbaked cake!

It was about the time that Imboden's line began to give way that Early personally arrived on the field. Sensing the potentially precarious situation and the possibility of a dangerous Federal thrust down the Salem Turnpike, he sent a courier racing rearward to bring forward Ramseur and his infantry. Johnston's brigade of that division was in the lead and exchanged fire with the advancing Federals. With a roar, the Confederate infantry rushed ahead onto the field and took over from Imboden's exhausted troopers. Seeing his infantry barreling forward, Early howled with glee. Turning his face toward the Federals he screamed that the Federals weren't facing any "buttermilk rangers" now, as he scathingly called all cavalry. The Union troopers came to a complete halt, fired a few shots at the oncoming Confederate ranks, and then began a slow deliberate retreat back to the area around the Quaker church.

There the Yankee command pondered the situation in the face of this new threat of unknown size. It had certainly become evident their foe was now no longer just cavalry but also some infantry regiments. Still there were some in the Federal ranks who wanted to continue the action but Averell felt that as darkness was setting in, it was best to halt. The day had not been a total failure for Averell. He had moved ahead as planned, driving the Rebel forces back on the city. Further, his casualties had been light; Hunter's chief of staff, Col. David

Strother, reported the casualties for the day at forty, but now darkness and an enemy of unknown strength had changed things.

While these events were transpiring on the main road from Liberty to Lynchburg, Hunter's other column, led by Duffié astride the Old Forest Road, was meeting with the same sequence of events. Covering that flank was McCausland with the two guns sent there earlier by Imboden. Duffié reported his first solid contact had been at 1:30 p.m. The enemy was deployed in very constricted woods through which the road ran. Duffié had to dismount his troopers. The scrap lasted for two hours before the Rebels grudgingly withdrew. Duffié then moved slowly forward, the sound of Averell's fight off to his right now audible. At a place called Clays Mill he halted his command and went into camp for the night, a distance he believed was approximately five miles from the city.[37]

As the sun went down Hunter and his staff moved into a nearby home that stood about a third of a mile west of the Quaker church. It had probably been picked out by his aides due to its proximity and the comfort it promised to offer. The name of the home was

Sandusky, built in 1808, became Hunter's headquarters and was one of the few large homes he did not burn. It is now being restored to its 1864 appearance.

Sandusky. Built in 1808, the builder had named it after the region in Ohio where Indians had held him captive during an exploration of that territory. But to the current owner, a retired US Army paymaster named Maj. George C. Hutter, the selection as Federal headquarters might well have caused some anxiety, considering Hunter's well-established reputation as a home burner. But, as it turned out, the two men knew each other in the old army as Hunter had also acted for a short time as a paymaster and both had served in the Mexican War. In any event, Hunter opted not to destroy Sandusky.

The mansion was a handsome brick structure of two stories sitting on high open ground that offered a good view of Early's defense line about two miles away. To obtain an even better view, Hunter's signal men found their way up into the attic and onto the roof. There, atop the roof, they had a panoramic view of the battlefield. The high perch was ideal for monitoring the battle and sending signals to Union commands. The house still stands today and is owned by the Historic Sandusky Foundation. It will serve as a Civil War museum and focal point for tours of Civil War Lynchburg.

With the coming of night, Hunter began spreading his maps in the Hutter parlor and conferring with aides and officers—two of whom were Col. Rutherford B. Hayes and Capt. William McKinley, both future presidents of the United States. Hunter later wrote that he had now learned that all the Confederate forces in the Valley and West Virginia areas were concentrated in Lynchburg under General Breckinridge and numbered about 10,000 -15,000, backed up with adequate artillery and strong earthworks.[38] To a reader of this report today, it would appear Hunter was not aware that much of Early's Corps was on the field that afternoon. Col. David Strother, his chief of staff, would later write that prisoners for Early's Corps had been taken and interrogated. While Hunter pondered this latest intelligence, a very tired Jubal Early also sought a suitable headquarters site and resting place. It is most likely he used his brother William's house in the city, a short ride from the new defense line. Before he turned in for the night, Early reviewed his troop status with his staff and commanders and made plans for the coming day.

It was now eight hours since the first trainload of Early's troops had arrived but the noise of moving trains had continued later that af-

Capt. William McKinley

Col. Rutherford B. Hayes

ternoon and on into the night. During those hours the noise that was reaching Hunter and his commanders' ears came from far more than the legendary switch engine and a few cars Early was alleged to have run in and out of the city. All afternoon and into the night trains were clattering about, arriving, switching, and then leaving the city. Early's switch engine may well have been active in the periods when there was no troop train activity, but his entire 8,000 man Corps and its supply trains had begun arriving about 1 p.m. and continued pouring into the city on into the darkness of June 17th. But the actual strength of all the Confederate forces confronting Hunter on the afternoon of the 17th could not have been more than 12,000, though this was unknown to Hunter. So Hunter pondered and Early waited, watching anxiously over his shoulder for the sound of trains that would signal the arrival of the rest of his II Corps.

CHAPTER 8

June 18th—Another Day of Battle

With dawn of June 18, both opposing commanders faced decisions. Hunter's mission to seize Lynchburg was becoming more complicated. During the night he and others of his command had clearly heard the noise of trains rattling in and out of Lynchburg. Confederate reinforcements were no doubt arriving, but how many? He contended that up until the morning of the 18th he had no positive intelligence that Lee had detached any considerable force to Lynchburg. He later wrote that he did not learn of Early's arrival with his full Corps until much later—about 2 p.m. of the 18th. So what were his relative strengths at that point? Further, his supply line was non-existent, severed once he left Lexington. He was living off the remnants of supplies he had begun the campaign with and what he had been able to glean from the unfriendly, and according to accounts of his quartermasters, not too plentiful countryside over which he had marched. There was no supply depot within supporting distance he could draw on. Of considerable concern to him was forage for his horses. Food for his troops was also in short supply.

Also of deep concern to Hunter was the report from his ordnance officers that ammunition was extremely tight. If he got into a large, drawn-out fight with the outcome in the balance there would be no resupply unless he captured the city quickly and then replenished from captured supplies. His artillery chief, Capt. Henry DuPont, was an able artilleryman and he had certainly seen to it that his guns had a respectable load of ammunition when they left Lexington—probably on the order of 150-200 rounds per gun. The ammunition was replenished at Staunton after the Piedmont fight and very little had been expended at Lexington. A supply train reached him at that place and artillery ammunition chests and infantry cartridge boxes were completely filled. From Lexington until

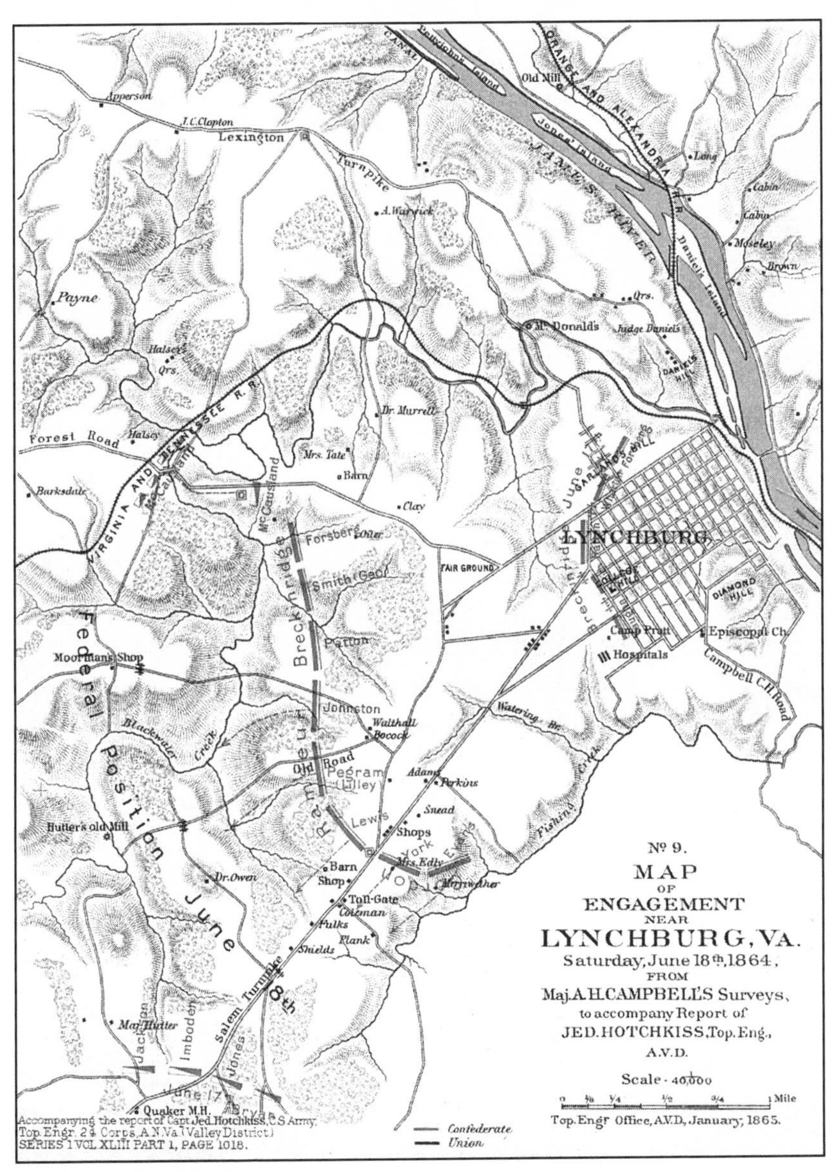

Approximate troop positions on the afternoon of June 18th

he had reached the outskirts of Lynchburg, there was only continuous skirmish fire, but not any full-fledged ammunition-exhausting fight. However, Hunter had severed his logistic ties when he left Lexington; there was no longer any resupply base close by. If there was to be an extended pitched battle, then his ammunition supply might pose a serious problem. So Hunter, with what Humphreys says was a "present for duty" strength of 16,643, saw a long, drawn-out battle as one he could not win.

What to do then? Hunter realized that he had three options: attack, stay put and await attack, or retreat. To attack required a strength that he felt could overcome the city's defenses. However, if indeed Early's Corps was arriving in the city in any great strength this would make an assault doubtful of success. To stay put was to give the enemy the initiative, with a force possibly growing superior to his. If the Confederates just let him sit it would only result in eventual retreat or surrender for lack of food and supplies, and this would mean failure of his mission—a failure that would certainly mean removal from command and disgrace. Immediate retreat meant the same. Thus a probing attack to test the enemy strength was chosen.

For Jubal Early that morning, his options were few. His primary mission was to defend the city. He was certainly aware that he was outnumbered—one source says Early's strength that morning was about 12,000. By now he had all of Ramseur's and probably most, if not all, of Gordon's division on hand but Rodes' division was yet to arrive. Even if Rodes arrived that morning this still left Early outnumbered. Yet that was nothing new to Confederate commanders and might readily be handled by good tactics, fighting from interior lines, and the benefit of earthworks. And, with his aggressive mind, Early must have given thought to keeping back some strength to lash out in counter-attack—if he could beat off Hunter's initial assault. Early probably advised his generals that this was in his mind, and it would be Gordon's division, and possibly Rodes' that he had in mind to use for this stroke—if the railroad moved Rodes there in time. So Early sat out on the lines at sun-up, watched and waited.

As dawn broke on June 18th, Hunter, in his official report, told of hearing during the night the distant noisy celebrations and rattling of trains, but states he still had no firm intelligence as to whether Lee had dispatched troops to defend Lynchburg. Lacking what he felt was hard intelligence, Hunter decided to push a swarm of skirmishers toward the enemy lines to test the defenses. In his report his wording states that he had by then been notified that the Old Forest Road to the west was also guarded by a strong redoubt. This would indicate that he had received word that Duffié had closed on the Fort McCausland area by midmorning. But Duffié had been moving slowly and certainly did not reach the Blackwater Creek line sooner than noon.

It was at 10:30 a.m. by his report that Hunter had sent a message to Duffié to attack on that flank. Concurrently, Averell was ordered to send two squadrons to the right to demonstrate in front of the Campbell County Court House Road. This force was shortly augmented by a brigade from Crook. It was about 11:00 a.m. when Sullivan's heavy skirmishing line began its firefight in the Fort Early area. According to Hunter this used up "the whole of the forenoon." But he had Sullivan's and the remainder of Crook's infantry divisions positioned so as to move either right or left of the Pike, to exploit the situation if a weak spot in the Confederate defense line was found. This done, Hunter then headed to the front to personally look for an opening between the two flanks or "redoubts" as he put it, through which he could hurl his infantry.

From a spot of elevated ground about three quarters of a mile in front of Fort Early he could have seen much of his front. This site was probably where today's Fort Avenue intersects with US 29 turning

West face of Fort Early, the only remaining intact fortification in Lynchburg.

to the left, or east. There were heavy patches of woodland but there was also much open ground, albeit terribly broken by steep ravines and steep hills. Through his field glasses Hunter determined that the redoubt and its flanking entrenchments directly in his front appeared too strong for a direct assault. But here Hunter came close to being personally hit by enemy fire. According to Captain DuPont, who was close by when Hunter and his party made this reconnaissance, the general and party rode ahead to the rise well within range and view of the Southern gunners. Instantly there was an outburst of cannon fire from the Rebel works. Shells screamed close by, just overhead, scattering the party into the woods on both sides of the road. DuPont remarked later that if the fire had been better aimed, it might have deprived the Federals of much of their battlefield high command. Even though the shells passed just overhead, DuPont was amazed at the accuracy of the Confederate gunners.[39]

There is some evidence that this artillery firing was done by Chapman's veteran battery. Other sources contend that Lieutenant Berkeley's two guns along with some pieces from Maj. Floyd King's battalion and two of Captain Douthat's Botetourt Artillery were involved. However, other evidence indicates that Douthat and Berkeley were at Fort McCausland.

As soon as the first salvo passed overhead, DuPont turned to Hunter and remarked that he felt these were new Confederate gunners; the people with whom they had been dealing earlier in the campaign could never have been that good with their first salvos. Hunter snorted that that was nonsense; the only guns in Lynchburg were those they had encountered at Piedmont, implying that those had been readily handled.[40]

Perhaps about 12:30 p.m., as Hunter scanned the horizon, a swarm of Rebel infantry suddenly poured out of their earthworks and headed directly toward him. It was sudden and totally unexpected. Sullivan's forward line, caught by surprise, retired rapidly. Alerted by the roar of gunfire, the rest of Sullivan's command began to deploy. What followed, however, is difficult to interpret and untangle. One has to rely primarily on Hunter's report written almost a month later. Crook's report is very brief about actions of the 18th, stating merely that after being sent to the right and returning he went into "position to support General Sullivan's division." Yet five of his regiments made reports that show they were in some heavy fighting, incurring over 200 casualties. The Official Records contain no report from Sullivan and none from any of his regiments. From Hunter's report, however, it is known that Sullivan was in action with the 116th Ohio Infantry of that command, cited for breaching the Confederate lines and planting its colors atop the earthworks. Hunter wrote that he believed Early was hitting the Federal center in the erroneous belief that Hunter had weakened the center with the extension of his lines. For a half hour the bitter scrap continued; then Crook's infantry came forward, deployed and moved forward. In the face of this threat the out-numbered Confederates fell back. For unknown reasons, Hunter failed to follow the Confederate withdrawal, but probably because he now believed most or all of Early's Corps was on the field and greatly outnumbered him.

Few Confederate reports survive but from interpreting post-war accounts and using logic, it seems that Early had made a spoiling attack, probably of brigade strength to keep Hunter off balance as well as to test his strength. If it shattered the enemy line Early would be ready to follow the old adage of reinforcing success and throw in additional strength. Apparently the Confederates made several other reconnaissances in force as they carried out what Hunter saw as several attempts to outflank him on his left. But the combined force of Sullivan and Crook proved too much. In a first hand account by a soldier in one of Ramseur's infantry regiments, the Federals, in what was apparently their counter-charge, reached a point about 150 yards from the Confederate line and then fell back in the face of the heavy enemy fire.

Behind the Union infantry lines DuPont's guns went into action with a heavy roar. DuPont had with him thirty-two guns (two pieces of unknown type but probably rifled guns detached to Averell's division). He quickly deployed these atop a ridge of high ground a few hundred yards in front of where Hunter had been, deploying them at very close intervals. This site is now marked on Fort Avenue by two tall, silver water towers. These guns, probably all rifled pieces (except for four Napoleons of Von Kleiser's battery that had lost two at New Market), now opened fire. The range to the Confederates, about 1,200 yards, was within the capability of all of DuPont's guns. The ground to the right of the gunners was thickly wooded according to DuPont, but the center and much of the left was largely open ground sloping toward the Confederate position. Soon a request came from General Crook for a battery of six guns, which reduced DuPont's gun total from thirty-two to twenty-six.

Confederate batteries positioned to oppose DuPont, according to Confederate participant Humphreys, were W. S. Lurty to the left or east side of Fort Early, George Chapman and William M. Lowry in or near the redoubt, Jackson a considerable distance farther to the Confederate right, and Douthat on the extreme right confronting Duffié. In reserve at the cemetery were two sections of Bryan's battery, which included two 20-pounder Parrotts and two rifled guns. These were a mish-mash of gun types, always a handicap, and those directly involved with DuPont were thus probably fewer in number, maybe sixteen in all. Still they held their own against DuPont's gunners. Humphreys noted that the total Confederate artillery strength available at Lynchburg was some forty guns that included Bryan's battery with six guns, Chapman with four, Lowry with four, Jackson-six, Lurty-four, McClanahan-six, Douthat-six, and Marquis (the Boy Battery)-four. Berkeley, apparently still in command of McClanahan's battery, had guns in Fort McCausland and two on the nearby Clifton Road site.[41] However, not all of these were involved in this action and none of the II Corps batteries reached Lynchburg in time to participate. However, a heavy artillery duel obviously occurred.

Sullivan's division did not break, but fell back slowly. However, the fight became prolonged and nasty. Sullivan's men continued to fall back slowly, and this move allowed some of DuPont's guns to get a partial enfilading fire on the advancing Confederates. Still, it was an alarming situation to Hunter, especially since prisoners had bragged about the presence of all of Early's Corps. Hunter thereupon sent a courier rushing to Crook, whom he had sent off to the right looking for a flanking spot, to return. As it happened, Crook had found the terrain abominable—a mass of deep ravines and precipitous rises as he moved toward Fishing Creek. There was no way any attacking units could keep any sort of formation or cohesion to outflank the Confederate left. Crook determined on his own to return to the center. He was on his way when Hunter's messenger reached him. The attacking Confederates now must have found Hunter's line a bit too strong and began a slow retirement to their own lines. About this time Crook's regiments, including the previously detached brigade, went into position behind Sullivan. While Hunter does not state he ordered an advance, one took place. Crook's regiments, along with Sullivan's, began to advance as the Rebel units had either come to a halt or had begun a slow retirement.

Col. Rutherford B. Hayes' 23rd Ohio of Crook's division chased back the Rebels in its front and contended they entered their lines, but that superior Rebel forces drove the bluecoats back "in some disorder." Similarly the 5th West Virginia of Crook's command moved from its position on the right or east side of the Turnpike across to the west side. From there it drove ahead through heavy woods for a half mile and then encountered a deep ravine, one that still exists today. This was the present-day area of Rhode Island and New Hampshire Avenues. Ahead was a steep hill atop where they saw a strong fortification, certainly Fort Early. The fire from there became so intense that the 5th West Virginia was forced to retire, suffering some thirty-five casualties. The 15th West Virginia also reported having been in the fight, coming out with losses totaling sixty-three. Both of these regiments were of Crook's command.[42]

The account of the 54th Pennsylvania, another of Crook's, is a little more detailed. This unit had been one of those detached earlier to accompany Averell's right flank reconnaissance but had returned about 11 a.m. At some point in time thereafter the regiment was ordered to advance. It crested a hill and marched down into an open field, where it came under heavy artillery fire. At the foot of the hill they found the Confederates "strongly posted in a deep ditch, concealed by thick weeds and underbrush, lining both banks." The Union regiment charged and drove their enemy backwards before halting behind a piece of rising ground that gave them shelter for the moment from Confederate fire. The 54th's line was now ragged and tired so the colonel paused to realign and rest the men. After about three minutes the 54th's commander yelled the command and the regiment resumed its advance.[43]

Over the crest it went. They quickly spotted the enemy about 200 yards ahead, behind what they said was "a stone wall, rail breastworks, and an old dwelling house, stable, and ice-house...." With a shout the regiment charged and drove the Confederates from their position. But it was here that the 54th suffered its heaviest casualties. So the unit halted, remaining "unmolested" until 9 p.m. that evening when orders came to retreat. The unit's official report noted that of some 420 men taken into action, eighty-five had become casualties, or 20 percent of its strength. Another of Crook's regiments, the 11th West Virginia, reported that it too went into action on the afternoon of the 18th under heavy artillery fire. The regiment, along with its sister regiments of the brigade, charged and drove the Confederates from their rifle pits. However, something happened on their right flank causing them to become exposed to a flanking fire. The 11th thereupon fell back thirty paces and reformed. It stayed here until nightfall until it too received the order to retreat. Sullivan's division was clearly in the fighting but no reports from him or any of his regiments exist in the Official Records. The only official record is Hunter's mention of the 116th Ohio entering the Rebel works on the 18th and planting its colors briefly atop the enemy earthworks. But additional proof of Early's arrival came to hand as Colonel Strother related in his diary that five North Carolinians had been captured by Sullivan's men and when questioned revealed they were from Early's newly arrived Corps.[44]

It was a clear but extremely hot day for the gunners of both sides as they sweated in the work about their pieces. All but one battery of DuPont's force were 3-inch rifled guns; the remaining unit was equipped with four smoothbore Napoleons. However, the effectiveness of both the relatively flat trajectory rifled cannon, as well as the Napoleons in counter-battery fire against Confederate units in the earthen fort, would have been extremely limited. The converse would have been true for the Confederate batteries. By his own statement, DuPont's batteries were at the start of the fight tightly packed and in open ground.

Even given the lack of precision gunnery and bursting effectiveness of Civil War artillery, a deployed field artillery battery, with over 120 horses, twelve limbers and six caissons, plus the six guns, made a large target area some 80 x 80 yards, hard to miss in counter-battery fire. Yet in DuPont's post-war account, there is no evidence of an official after-action report by him, and he makes no mention of any very damaging fire. Unfortunately, only two batteries made reports and both indicate that there was considerable redeployment once the fight started. One unit, the 1st Kentucky battery, reported some five wheels damaged, an axle splintered, a trail spike shot away, as well as one horse killed and five wounded. The other unit that made a report was the 1st Ohio Battery. It reported heavy firing, but sustained only four men lightly wounded. The artillery of both sides, while making much noise, rendered few casualties due to the inadequacies of the material of that day and the primitive fire direction systems.

At one point in the artillery duel, Bryan's Confederate reserve sections were told that they were desperately needed to replace a unit in the vicinity of Fort Early. It turned out that this was not so, but Bryan's men set out from the cemetery as fast as the ground would permit. They followed a road eastward, just south of the cemetery that led down to a little stream. Where the road crossed the stream was the northern end of a long hill that ran north from where there stood an asylum of sorts. The hill was bare and sloped gently to the west, its foot joining that of the hill on which Lewis's brigade of Ramseur's division was posted. On its east side there was an almost vertical bluff at the base of which ran a railroad. East of this hill was a much higher one that was lightly timbered and here he saw Confederate infantry in position.

Bryan's four guns arrived at the bare area of the hill or ridge, the cannon being manhandled to the top. They were then moved southward along the ridge for about two-hundred yards. At that point they were square on the right flank of the Federal artillery some 1,000 yards distant. This site is probably near today's City Stadium. From here they opened fire on a Federal battery in the southeast corner of a grove of trees, which hid them from all but Bryan's guns. A fierce gun duel then began. One of Bryan's guns, a 20-pounder, began what was called "stripping" its shells so they failed to rotate and went astray. What was happening was probably the shells were prematurely stripping off their expanding base or sleeve that enables the projectile to bite the rifling of the gun as it speeds out of the tube. The projectile then, lacking its stabilizing rifling, simply rattled and flew inaccurately. Shortly thereafter a staff officer arrived to tell Bryan to pull the 20-pounder out of action. It was then three Confederate guns versus eight to ten Federals. At that point both sides slackened their fire and Bryan's men began digging emplacements for their guns. Bryan's men later claimed to have been the ones who shot up the 1st Kentucky Battery, forcing it to use all but one of its spare wheels.[45]

About 2:00 p.m. Hunter stated the heavy firing wound down. It was also the time he stated he received final reports from prisoner interrogation that his opponent really was Jubal Early; his Corps, allegedly with 20,000 men, was on hand. To Hunter's mind this would mean he was thoroughly out-numbered. Also worrisome was that some of his units were reporting their ammunition almost gone. To Hunter it was time to bring things to a halt and take stock of their situation. Hunter backed off from any further combat and Early's tired men sat down to rest as Early planned his next move.

CHAPTER 9

Union Failure on the Left Flank

Simultaneously on the 18th with the main action in front of Fort Early, Duffié's force, far off to Hunter's left, was not helping matters. Complaints had been made earlier in the campaign that Duffié did not maintain proper communications with the main force, and this seems to have continued on the 17th and 18th. Duffié reported that he had dispatched messengers, but the rugged and mountainous terrain over which his command had been operating for the past ten days resulted in his messengers either getting lost or captured. In any event, Hunter and Averell rarely knew where he was. And, to reconstruct Duffié's action for the balance of the 17th and all day of the 18th poses a difficult problem—trying to sort out facts from his report that disagree with other details.

On the morning of the 18th, he moved his command slowly forward along the Old Forest Road, having skirmishes with McCausland's troops at every turn. Up to this time he maintains he received no orders from Hunter. About 9:00 a.m. his troopers had bumped into an enemy contingent guarding a bridge over a railroad, probably the same site as the current bridge just past the intersection of Old Forest Road and US 501 North. Duffié said this was four miles from the city. A brisk fight broke out while the Confederates tried to set the road bridge on fire. But Duffié's men were able to force their opponents back before the structure was totally destroyed. Crossing over, the column resumed its march. It was about 10:30 a.m. when he received a message from Averell, probably a duplicate of the earlier one, stating that Hunter wanted him to attack vigorously.

After reading the order, Duffié called his brigade commanders to him and issued new orders. The advance would proceed in three columns; Col. R. F. Taylor's brigade was to march on the right side of the Old Forest Road; an artillery section, two guns under a lieutenant, and a regiment of cavalry would move along the road; and Col. L. Wynkoop's brigade along the left side of the road. Shortly thereafter the columns began to advance again, with flankers out front and on both sides.

It was just minutes later when the Confederate troopers opened fire again from behind some rail barricades. The Federal skirmishers pushed ahead and the Confederates retired once more. Duffié's troopers advanced forward another two miles. At that point they found the Confederates had retired beyond a bridge crossing Blackwater Creek. Duffié's skirmishers, pressing closely, found the approaches to the stream swampy and the banks very steep. His entire command, he reported, was then deployed and moved forward to within a half mile of the fortifications.

Directly ahead, they could see that the roadway and the bridge were commanded by what Duffié reported as two fortifications: Fort McCausland, with probably two guns of Douthat's battery and perhaps two to four others from a different command, and the second "fort" being simply Douthat's two guns to the left rear of that fort and in some sort of earthwork (see map below). These guns covered the Old Forest Road approach from the west as well as a trail, now Langhorne Road, that led down from the Lexington Road to the north, now Rivermont Avenue, to the bridge and a mill close by.

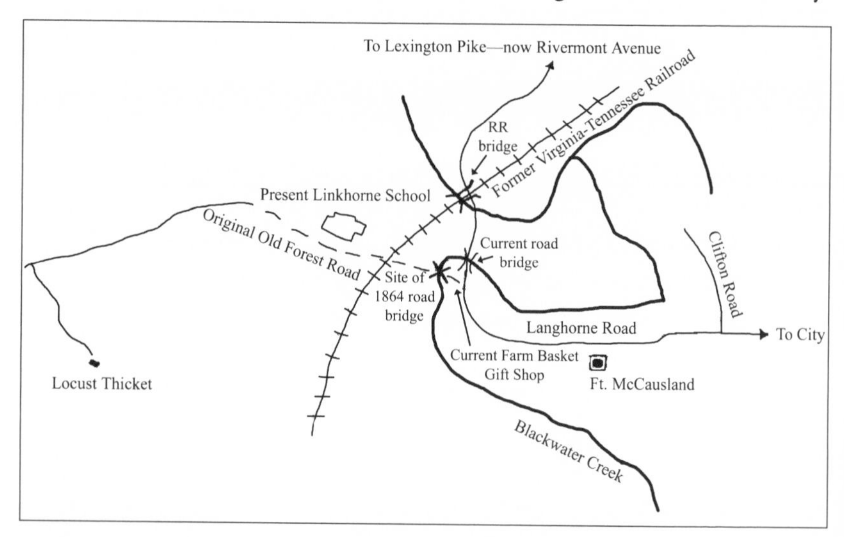

Area of Duffié's feeble effort

Duffié immediately deployed his troops. From these fortifications came a steady burst of cannon fire. Duffié yelled for the lieutenant and his two guns to begin counter-battery fire.[46] According to one source the guns that did the most firing against Duffié were the two 3-inch rifles from the Botetourt Artillery positioned to the right rear of Fort Early and two 6-pounder smoothbores and two 12-pounder howitzers within the fort.

At this point Duffié reported he ordered a general advance of all of his skirmishers. The 1st New York (Lincoln) Cavalry was ordered to move ahead on the left of the line, crossing Blackwater Creek. Additionally, two squadrons of the 20th Pennsylvania Cavalry were ordered to charge the bridge, but were driven back by what Duffié described as heavy infantry fire. The New Yorkers, however, supposedly held on across the far side of the creek bank until they were driven back by a Confederate attack about 5:00 p.m. There were also a few weak demonstrations by Duffié's troopers later that afternoon and early in the evening of which one was repulsed by infantry in wooded ground across Blackwater Creek.

Then someone reported a cloud of dust off to Duffié's left. A column of enemy cavalry was spotted approaching. Two graycoat squadrons from Wynkoop's command were sent to hold them in check, which Duffié reported as successful—the enemy seen to be retiring. This was no doubt a reconnaissance party sent out by the commander at Fort McCausland; perhaps Elzey or Ransom had arrived by this time to ensure the Confederate right flank was secure. Finding no Federal effort brewing in that quarter, the force retired. Then Duffié received a report of enemy forces overlapping his right. A regiment from Taylor's brigade was sent in that direction. Directly ahead Taylor was convinced he could see Confederate reinforcements approaching.

It was now 5:00 p.m. by Duffié's timing and the enemy opened a heavy fire that forced the men of the 1st New York back. To add to Duffié's assumed worries, General Taylor now was sure he could hear whistles of arriving trains along with band music. He was correct, as more of Early's units were arriving. Duffié, too, was now convinced he was opposed by a vastly superior force.

It was at this time that Duffié sent a message to Hunter telling him that he had carried out his order and attacked, at 12:30, making two charges on the enemy fortifications that had developed the enemy's full strength, believed to be much superior to his. He also reported that Confederate forces were trying to turn to his right, which he would attempt to meet. However, he continued, he had no contact with Averell.

At 7:00 p.m. came a message from Averell stating that an infantry brigade from Crook's division was coming to Duffié's aid and that Duffié was to attack in concert with this force. This message was no doubt in reply to Duffié's earlier message, but the courier of that communication had gotten lost in the rugged terrain between the two wings. However, minutes later came a messenger from Hunter telling him that the entire army was retiring; orders would be sent advising him of the timing of the moves. Duffié thereupon took it upon[47] himself to disregard the attack order and stay put, his ammunition being exhausted.

There are wide discrepancies, however, between what Duffié reported and other evidence. Here is what really seems to have happened. So wooded is some of the ground today, and so developed by shopping centers and housing over the entire battle area, that to try to see the land as it was at that time is extremely difficult. Old Forest Road, the route Duffié was using, today is basically the same as it was in 1864 except for the last part. Today it turns hard right at the Forest Hill Shopping Center. In 1864 Old Forest Road continued straight ahead, through rolling, but open ground of the Halsey farm. It reached a point where the present road, now called Linkhorne Drive, bends sharply to the left, and directly ahead is the Linkhorne School complex.

The original Old Forest roadbed, still visible as a gully, passed just to the right of this school complex, for about a quarter-mile, where it descended down a steep incline, crossed the railroad bed of what was then the Virginia and Tennessee line, now an abandoned stretch of the Norfolk-Western, to a small bridge over Blackwater Creek. The stone remains of that old bridge can be seen today from behind the Farm Basket gift shop complex on the right or east bank of the creek. At that point it joined the trail that came down from the Lexington Road to the north and a road that led to Halsey's mill and then into the city past Fort McCausland. The present bridge is about 100 yards

Abutments to the original bridge across Blackwater Creek behind where the Farm Basket is located today.

downstream from that point, close to the now abandoned railroad trestle and Ivy Creek that here flows into Blackwater Creek. At the point where the present day road turns right at a stop light in front of the Kings Island restaurant, to the south of the road, perhaps 300 yards back, stands a colonial era white frame home named Locust Thicket. Tradition says that Duffié used this structure as his headquarters during the day and night of June 18th.

But to better understand the possible actions here it is important to look at the lay of the land. The ground around the Locust Thicket area is a bit higher than the ground where Fort McCausland is located—800 feet versus 700 feet. The range from Fort McCausland to the Locust Thicket area is some 2,000 yards. However, the ground to the east drops slightly to the vicinity of the school, then to the Halsey Farm, and at that point is about the same elevation as the fort. The range to that point from the fort is around 1,500 yards. Therefore, artillery from Fort McCausland could not see any troop movement in the Locust Thicket area. Not until the column reached the school vicinity would they come in view. Further, unless the guns in the fort were rifled pieces, advancing Federal troops in the Locust Thicket area were beyond effective smoothbore range, particularly if any of the fort's guns were old 6-pounder smoothbores, and there may have been two. But even if they were rifles, flat trajectory weapons would not be capable of bringing accurate fire to bear until the target reached the Halsey farm. So it would appear that gunfire from the fort did not erupt until Duffié's column reached the farm or perhaps not until he tried to have several of his units cross Blackwater Creek. From Linkhorne School to the fort was well within the effective range of any smoothbore gun, including 6-pounders as well as the two rifled guns to the right rear of the main fort.

Confusing the matter, however, is the report that Duffié first tangled with the Confederates somewhere in the vicinity of the Locust Thicket house. Evidence of this are alleged bullet holes in some of the walls of the house and several canister round balls reportedly recovered from the grounds—a type of round fired only at ranges from 400 yards and closer. A burn scar exists in the parlor of that house, and legend says this was caused by a careless Union trooper rolling a blazing log out of the fireplace in the parlor onto the beautiful pine floors, leaving a scorched mark. Legend also says Duffié used the room di-

Locust Thicket

This 1805 house allegedly served as Duffié's headquarters on June 18th. Canister balls and Minie bullets were recently found in the yard.

rectly to the right of what was then the front door as his headquarters. Today the house is in private hands and is well preserved.

Duffié probably encountered a heavy outpost line there that the commander at Fort McCausland, either Wharton, McCausland, or Elzey, had sent forward. The defenders may have included some guns or more likely the light howitzers that had been with McCausland and Imboden from the start. McCausland's men were, along with Wharton's division, holding the right end of Early's position. If the evidence of battle around the house, to include the canister balls recovered, is accepted as fact, then this line had forced Duffié to deploy again. What probably followed was a slow retrograde move by the Confederates, moving back from ridge to low ridge, until finally reaching the area of the Linkhorne School, then the Halsey Farm. At this point they retired down the old roadway, across the bridge that no longer stands, and up into the Fort McCausland defense positions.

But the main discrepancy with Duffié's account comes from the post-war published unofficial narrative of the 1st New York (Lincoln) Cavalry. No action of any kind is mentioned as happening with that unit on the 18th other than searching for water and trying to burn a bridge, the exact location of which is confusing.[48] An action of the size and intensity described by Duffié would certainly have been mentioned in such a unit history. The account recorded its casualties for June 18th as zero, whereas at New Market and Piedmont they had suffered on the heavy side—99 and 26 respectively.

So Duffié's action on the 18th was probably limited to some sporadic long range shelling by his two guns and scattered exchange of fire from the bluffs by his troopers and the Confederates in and around the fort until what he saw as enemy reinforcements put an end to his "offensive." About all that can be stated in fact about the action here was that Duffié's troopers did some ineffective long range shooting with their carbines at Confederate infantry in earthworks across the creek while Confederate artillery in Fort McCausland and on Clifton Road fired at Duffié's two guns and any perceived movement by the Union troopers toward the bridge. The 15th New York Cavalry did report in its unofficial account of the battle that it suffered a total of thirty-two men to all causes.

Confirming Duffié's lack of aggressiveness is the account in Colonel Tibbitts' diary. His unit, the 21st New York Calvary, was in the forefront all day, but his men, according to his diary, only exchanged fire with the Confederate skirmishers across the creek and fired at the gun crews of what he said were five artillery pieces. And, judging by the amount of return fire, Tibbitts believed there were some 2,500 infantry facing him—probably not a bad estimate. Also of interest is his entry stating that Averell sent orders to him four times not to cross and become engaged. His diary further reflects the confusion and lack of command and control in Hunter's army. When he received the order to retire he could not locate the rest of the brigade. He finally found it only to learn the army was retreating. Once again the brigade moved off and the colonel and unit were left behind "in strange country with very little knowledge of the woods and not knowing where the brigade had gone."[49]

The bottom line of the action on the Confederate right seems to have been little more than some sporadic shelling between Duffié's two guns and those of the Confederate engaged in counter-battery firing as well as deterring the half-hearted attempt to approach the bridge over Blackwater Creek. There was also some long-range small-arms fire between some of the cavalrymen and mounted infantry of McCausland's command along with firing by regiments of Breckinridge's division. The firing must not have been heavy for such accounts that do exist make no mention of any heavy fighting in this quarter. Oddly, such papers available of Confederate General Wharton and Colonel Patton, both brigade commanders, make no mention of action on this day. There are no reports by either officer in the Official Records. And there is still the lingering question as to whether Wharton was in command of his brigade or whether it was Colonel Forsberg. However, according to an account by the latter, written many years after the war, Forsberg was in command.[50]

There is an interesting account about the actions surrounding Douthat's two guns on Clifton Road. According to an account written in 1922 in the *Confederate Veteran*, No. 32, by Adam H. Pleckert, a veteran of Douthat's battery, the battery was put in position with its two 6-pounder smoothbore guns and the two 12-pounder howitzers on what he called the Forest Road. The other two guns, 3-inch rifled pieces, were on what he termed the Turnpike. Apparently Pleckert's memory concerning the road names had become confused over the years. Other evidence places the four guns in the vicinity of Fort McCausland, just south of what is today Langhorne Road, not Forest Road. Here they were in support of the infantry thereabouts. The two rifled guns under a Lieutenant Oberchain were located across Langhorne Road on a ridge near a soap stone quarry about three quarters of a mile from the Virginia and Tennessee railroad bridge. The site was probably just a few yards north from Langhorne Road on what is today Clifton Road. From here Pleckert said the two pieces kept driving back Duffié's troopers who were striving to burn the railroad bridge to their front. In actuality what they were apparently doing was not only chasing off Duffié's feeble burning attempts but also firing at some of Duffié's dismounted troopers trying to cross the wagon and foot bridge lower down the slope that was an extension of Forest Road.

Pleckert's account states that during the firing, one of the 3-inch guns blew up. The lieutenant thereupon withdrew the damaged gun and, along with its crew, headed back into the city to find a replacement. There is some question here as to the cause of the gun's disablement. The author's life-long study of Civil War artillery never

Site of Bryan's two-gun section off Clifton Road across from Fort McCausland. Railroad bridge and road bridge in the distance.

revealed an incident of a wrought iron 3-inch rifle blowing up. With the cast iron Parrott guns, such a malfunction was all too common. Whatever the cause, it is fairly certain that one gun went out of action at a critical time.

According to Pleckert's account, the lieutenant quickly reached the city and found a gun park. As the battery had been in Lynchburg for several days, it is quite probable that the lieutenant or some other battery person had noted the presence of the gun park in the supply-laden city. At that point Lieutenant F. G. Oberchain politely but firmly demanded a replacement gun from the officer in charge. That officer contended that Oberchain would have to search out the appropriate officer and get a proper requisition. Oberchain then bluntly told the man that the gun was urgently needed, time was critical, the Yankees might well get into the city if he did not get that gun to stop them; that he had come for a gun and did not intend to leave without one. With that he saluted, told the officer to bill it to the Botetourt Artillery, told his men to seize one, and back to the fight the unit went.

In another version, the gun suffered a broken wheel and it was Capt. H. C. Douthat who took his crew into the city in search of a replacement. In this version Douthat encountered the stubborn supply officer and, then losing patience, pulled his pistol and told the officer that this was his requisition, had his men seize a gun, and returned with it to the fight. Whatever the precise details, it can be reasonably certain that for a short time the defenses along Langhorne Road were one gun short, possibly critically short had Duffié pushed forcefully ahead.

The day had not been an outstanding one for any of Hunter's efforts. He had suffered a bloody repulse in front of Fort Early and had had to pull back. Efforts to turn the Confederate right had failed. On the Confederate left, terrain had doomed action in that area. Now came increasing reports about the arrival of all of Early's vaunted II Corps. As sundown approached it was not a hopeful situation for Hunter.

Exactly where the respective commanders had their headquarters posts on June 18th is unknown. Hunter probably located himself behind the woods known to exist to the east or right of the Pike, near where he had made his reconnaissance earlier. This location would have given him some protection, a site couriers could readily find, and be midway between his main striking divisions. As for Early, at some point he was certainly in the vicinity of Fort Early, probably at the time he launched Ramseur's spoiling attack. Prior to that he may well have moved himself out of his brother's house in the city to a site closer to the front. This might have been a large frame house that became known as the McWane house.

This house, which still stands, albeit greatly changed in appearance, is located on a piece of high open ground about 400 yards to the right rear of Fort Early. It was a rather large structure on a site well located, about midway along Early's long line. The house is known to have been struck by at least one Federal cannon shell that passed through a window shutter. Whether there were other shell hits is now lost in time. But the house would have been within sight of and range of the Federal guns. Perhaps some sharp-eyed Yankee gun crew spotted activity there and had flung some rounds in that direction. It may never be known. The shell-pierced shutter that existed for many years has since disappeared.[51]

CHAPTER 10

The Finale

On the evening of June 18th the opposing commanders planned their next moves. Hunter now saw that he could not accomplish his task. Averell had reported encountering a large body of enemy cavalry on the Federal right, and Duffié had likewise reported, erroneously as it would turn out, that heavy enemy reinforcements were threatening his position to the left. Intelligence indicated the enemy in strength opposite the Federal center. Hunter believed the Confederates were double his strength and well supplied and he was receiving reports that there was not enough ammunition to sustain another well-contested battle. The die was quickly cast in Hunter's mind; he had no choice but retreat, being he was heavily outnumbered, his ammunition supply dangerously down, his supplies beginning to run low, and no hope of any reinforcements or additional supplies and ammunition. In the face of all of this, orders went out for the trains to retire immediately by the Pike; the combat elements were to begin pulling out at dark heading for Liberty, now Bedford. As he faced about, Hunter must have realized his campaign was a failure, but, as he would reveal to all in his later writings, no part of the blame did he see as resting on his shoulders; he felt others were to blame!

With the onset of dark, the troop retirement began. Only a strong picket line was left in place to discourage any probing by the enemy. At midnight this force was to withdraw. Hunter boasted that this withdrawal was accomplished with no loss of men or material. He did admit that he was forced to leave behind "a few wounded" by mistake. But that statement is refuted by one of his own men who contended that some 150 wounded were left, along with one surgeon, as they were too sick to be moved. The next day a Confederate surgeon arrived and found in the barn and on the grounds of Sandusky about 100 very badly wounded Federals, of which he felt five might recover.

One amusing incident happened here on the 19th. Some of the VMI cadets asked permission to visit the hospital. One of these was Cadet Carter H. Harrison. Given the okay, Harrison walked about. While strolling down the lanes of wounded he stopped suddenly. On the socks of one of the prone Federals he saw the monogrammed letters "C. H. H." He recognized them immediately—they were a pair his grandmother had knitted for him. Further inspection revealed the man's underclothing was also Harrison's! Furious, Carter called for a surgeon. The Yankee contended he had bought the items in Lexington. Harrison refused to believe that story, telling one and all that the items had obviously been looted from his trunk in barracks when the Federals were ransacking it prior to setting it afire. Carter had the garments and socks removed and returned to his possession.

As for Early, he was not disposed that night to undertake a major attack on the 19th until he felt sure his entire Corps would be available. He was not sure of Hunter's next move, but added a bit of muscle to his right. During the night of the 18th and19th, Early brought over from their bivouac in the city cemetery into Fort McCausland the VMI cadet battalion, armed with their new British Enfield rifle muskets. It had been an extremely dark night and Col. Scott Shipp, commanding the battalion of cadets, had ordered each cadet to place his hand on the cartridge box of the cadet in front as they made their way into the fort. It was a miserable march for the young cadets as they moved in directed silence into the fort. They found the newly dug fort a mass of wet stiff red clay soon pounded into dough. As one cadet later described things, "The place was horrible...There was no place to lie down. All a man could do was sit plump down in the mud, his gun across his lap...I could not resist peeping over the parapet, and there, but a short distance from us, in a little valley, were the smoldering camp-fires of the enemy...never doubting that there would be work for us at daybreak."[52]

Unaware of Hunter's poor logistical situation, Early was hesitant to believe that the Yankee commander was ready to give up. Then, sometime after midnight, word came that the Yankee army was moving, but in what direction? Perhaps Hunter was flanking him, looking for an opening, or moving along the river, heading toward Grant at Petersburg. It was apparently not until some time in the early morning darkness of June 19th, that he learned Hunter was falling back toward Liberty. Then Early gave orders to pursue.

Hunter went into camp seven miles east of Liberty on the 19th and went into camp. Early's pursuit was a bit slow, his soldiers were equally exhausted. However, the leading Rebels under General Ramseur caught up with Hunter's rear guard late that afternoon and drove it back onto the main body. The 8th Ohio Cavalry, acting as guard, suffered seventy-nine killed and wounded when darkness ended the scrap. It was not until 4 p.m. the next day, as the Federals neared Buford's Gap, that the Rebels again appeared for another rear guard action. At Salem, Virginia, was another rear guard fight during which, according to the 15th New York Cavalry account, Hunter lost eight guns and had to destroy a large part of his remaining ammunition to prevent its capture. But here the pursuit basically ended and Hunter's army was able to march back into West Virginia, and, as for Hunter, into military oblivion.

Casualties in the fighting at Lynchburg are hard to determine accurately. One thing that can be said is that there was no bloodletting of the sort seen at Sharpsburg or Cold Harbor. The *Official Records* list Hunter's casualties from all causes for the period June 10-23 at 938. Confederate losses are more difficult to substantiate. One study by a local historian puts their losses at around 300, which is probably close to reality.

But of far greater significance was the repulse of the threat to the vital base of Lynchburg. General Lee had proven again to be a master strategist. Faced with an overwhelming army at Petersburg, he had quickly recognized the urgent need to save Lynchburg and he took a desperate chance, virtually splitting his outnumbered army. But he had taken desperate chances before such as Second Manassas and at Chancellorsville. So he gambled that he could survive by the valor and skill of those who remained, that he could hold off any attack, and thus sent almost a third of his army on a far-ranging mission. Early's belligerent defense of the city had shattered Hunter's belief that the plum was his for the picking. Instead of plum, however, he found a very prickly thorn bush.

Elated at the news of Hunter's defeat and retreat, the people of Lynchburg whooped and hollered. Everyone who had had a part or even claimed to have had a role, was the recipient of much praise—railroad personnel, the wounded from the hospital, nurses, doctors, the militia, the VMI cadets, and, of course, Early and his men. On June 24th, the city passed a formal resolution commending one and all for "their timely and efficient services in driving the enemy from our borders."

Further, McCausland was singled out for his skillful delaying tactics and his subsequent hammering of Hunter during his retreat at a place called Hanging Rock. A committee came together and raised $3,000 and purchased a beautiful engraved sword and a pair of silver spurs for the general as a reward for his services. The sword, its belt, and brass Virginia crested buckle now belong to the Lynchburg City Museum. One of the two spurs was lost in 1865, but the surviving one is today in the hand of his heirs.

Early's victory at Lynchburg was not only successful, but was the beginning of an offensive into northern land. Early chased the retreating Hunter and his beaten army out of the Valley back across the mountains into West Virginia, and to all intents, Hunter and his army were out of the war for the time being. Then, with his vaunted II Corps, albeit a shadow of its Jackson days, Early marched down the Valley to threaten the Federal capital—a constant worry of the Lincoln administration throughout the war. Frantic wires were sent to Grant, who was forced to drain off men from Lee's front. The two moves collectively probably gave the Confederacy another six months of life, but at a heavy cost in men's lives and really to no end. Thankfully, in that sense, it would all end a few months later at Appomattox Court House on April 9th of 1865.

Facing immense criticism for the lost opportunity at Lynchburg, Hunter resigned his command and was replaced by Gen. Philip Sheridan. Yet in an amazing move, Hunter was brevetted—a form of honorary promotion in rank—a reward for outstanding service, for the Piedmont victory and the Valley Campaign—a campaign that eventually all would later see as a fiasco. But Hunter contended no fault on his part for the failure in front of Lynchburg; he claimed later that it was Averell's fault that he did not take the city, that

Sullivan was worthless, and Duffié was hopeless. Only Crook elicited any praise from Hunter. Earlier Hunter had served in 1863 on the infamous court martial of Gen. FitzJohn Porter. Following Lincoln's assassination in 1865, he presided over the trial of Lincoln conspirators. He accompanied Lincoln's body to Springfield, Illinois. With the coming of peace, he faded into obscurity, his reputation as a ruthless pyromaniac remains as his greatest legacy for his personal history.

Jubal Early also survived the war, returning to Lynchburg to practice law. A bachelor all of his life, he also retained his reputation for being cantankerous and outspoken. No one ever questioned his military skills, though he would become embroiled in post-war acrimony with a number of his contemporaries. He died in 1894 at 78 years of age and was buried in Lynchburg with much pomp and ceremony. Bands, generals, politicians, veterans and the full Corps of Cadets from VMI participated in his funeral. Today his grave and tall monument sit atop a high knoll in the Spring Hill Cemetery in a fitting view of the place of his victory over Hunter.

Tomb of
General Jubal A. Early
Spring Hill Cemetery
Lynchburg, Virginia

END NOTES

1. Early, Jubal A. *Memoirs: Autobiographical Sketch and Narrative of the War Between the States*. Baltimore, 1989, cited hereafter as *Autobiography: A Memoir of the Last Year of the War for Independence in the Confederate States of America.* Lynchburg, 1867, cited hereafter as *Memoir.*

2. Ibid.

3. Ibid.

4. Bean, W. G. *Sandie Pendleton*. Chapel Hill, 1959. p. 204.

5. U. S. War Department. *War of the Rebellion: A Compilation of the Official Records*, Series II. Hereafter cited as O. R. My source for these was a CD. Thus it was extremely difficult to transpose to page numbers. Thus I have not included these but identified the report. All citations are in Vol. XXXVII, pt. 1; *Ibid.*

6. Duncan, Richard R. *Lee's Endangered Left.* Baton Rouge, 1998. p. 266.

7. O. R.*; Memoir; Autobiography.*

8. Ibid.

9. Ibid.

10. Ibid.

11. Ibid.

12. Houck, Peter W. *Confederate Surgeon: The Recollections of E. A. Craighill.* Lynchburg, 1988; *A Prototype of a Confederate Hospital Center*, Lynchburg, 1986.

13. O. R. Hunter's Official Report.

14. Boatner, Mark M. *The Civil War Dictionary*, New York, 1991. pp. 418-419. Cited hereafter as Boatner.

15. Ibid. p. 817.

16. Ibid. p. 209.

17. Ibid. p. 35.

18. Ibid. pp. 250-251; *North-South Magazine*, April 2002.

19. DuPont, Henry A. *The Campaign in the Valley of Virginia and the Expedition to Lynchburg*. New York, 1925. Cited hereafter as DuPont.

20. Humphreys, Andrew A. *Campaigns of the Civil War: The Virginia Campaign of 1864 and 1865*. Edison, NJ 2002. Cited hereafter as *Humphreys*. This is an extremely valuable narrative as the author was a participant in the Lynchburg engagement.

21. *Memoir*; *Autobiography*; Davis, William C. *Breckinridge: Statesman, Soldier, Symbol*. Baton Rouge, 1974. P.441.

22. Humphreys.

23. Pauley, Michael J. *Unreconstructed Rebel: The Life and Times of General John McCausland, CSA*. Charleston, 1992. Cited hereafter as Pauley.

24. Bonnell, John C. *Sabres in the Shenandoah: The 21st New York Cavalry, 1863-1866*. Shippensburg, 1996; Walker, Gary. *Hunter's Fiery Raid Through Virginia Valleys*. Roanoke, 1989. Cited hereafter as Walker.

25. Tibbitts, William B. Diary of Col. Tibbitts, Tibbitts Family Collection, Manuscripts and Special Collections, New York State Archives, Albany; Bonnell, op. cit.

26. Pauley, op. cit.

27. Swisher, James K. *Warrior in Gray*. Shippensburg. 2000.

28. Boatner, op. cit. P. 348.

29. Forsberg Manuscript at Leyburn Library, W & L University, Lexington, VA.

30. O. R. Hunter's Report.

31. Walker, op cit.

32. *Memoir: Autobiography.* Op. cit.

33. O. R. Averell's and Duffié's Reports.

34. Blackford, Charles M. *Campaign and Battle of Lynchburg.* Lynchburg, VA, 1994. pp. 22 -23.

35. O. R. Averell's Report.

36. Ibid., Reports of the 91st Ohio, 12th Ohio, 14th West Virginia.

37. Ibid., O. R. Duffié's Report.

38. Ibid., Hunter's Report

39. DuPont, op. cit.

40. Ibid.

41. Humphreys, op. cit.

42. O. R. Reports of Crook and the 23d Ohio, 5th West Virginia, and 15th West Virginia.

43. O. R. Report of the 54th Pennsylvania.

44. Ibid., Report of the 11th West Virginia

45. Humphreys, op. cit.

46. O. R. Duffié's Report.

47. Ibid. Timing in Civil War accounts is very subjective. The author has encountered differences up to four hours for the same incident.

48. Bonnell, op. cit.

49. Tibbitts op. cit.

50. Forsberg

51. Chambers, S. Allen, Jr. *Lynchburg: An Architectural History.* Charlottesville, 1981, p. 422.

52. Report of VMI Superintendent Francis H. Smith to Maj. Gen. William H. Richardson, June 17, 1864, copy in VMI Archives; Cooper, William. *One Hundred Years at V.M.I.*, Richmond, 1939, Vol. III, pp. 46-47.

SUGGESTED READINGS

Note: Any thorough study of the American Civil War requires the use of the "ORs" — *The War of the Rebellion: Official Records,* printed by the War Department. Series I encompasses most of the official after-action reports and Vol. 37 of this series carries reports of the Lynchburg Campaign.

Black, Robert C. *Railroads of the Confederacy.* 1952. Chapel Hill.

Blackford, Charles M. *Campaign and Battle of Lynchburg.* 1994. Warwick House, Lynchburg, VA.

Bonnel, John C. *Sabres in the Shenandoah - The 21st New York Cavalry.* 1996. Burd Street Press, Shippensburg, PA.

Casler, John O. *Four Years in the Stonewall Brigade.* 1893. Guthrie, OK.

Cooper, William C. *One Hundred Years at V. M. I.* 1939. Garrett Massie, Richmond, VA.

Craighill, Edley. "Lynchburg, Virginia in the War Between the States". *Historical Sketches From The Iron Worker.* Lynchburg. 1984.

Duncan, Richard R. *Lee's Endangered Left.* 1998. Louisiana State University Press, Baton Rouge, LA.

DuPont, Henry A. *The Campaign of 1864 in The Valley of Virginia.* 1925. National Americana, New York.

Early, Jubal A. "A Memoir of the Last Year of the War for Independence", 1866. Pamphlet, 2nd edition. Copy in Jones Library, Lynchburg, VA.

Early, Lt. Gen. Jubal A. *A Narrative of the War Between the States.* 1989. DeCapo Press, New York.

Humphreys, Milton W. *A History of the Lynchburg Campaign.* 1924. University of Virginia Press, Charlottesville, VA.

Morris, George and Susan Foutz. *Lynchburg in The Civil War.* 1984. H. E. Howard, Inc. Lynchburg, VA.

Osbourne, Charles VC. *Jubal—The Life and Times of General Jubal A. Early, CSA.* 1992. Louisiana State University Press, Baton Rouge, LA.

Pauley, Michael J. *Unreconstructed Rebel: The Life of General John McCausland, CSA.* 1992. Pictorial Histories, Charleston, WVA.

Robertson, James I. *The Stonewall Brigade.* 1963. Louisiana State University Press, Baton Rouge, LA.

Strother, David H. (Porte Crayon). "An Eye-Witness Account of the Battle of Lynchburg." 1960. *The Iron Worker*, Spring 1960. Lynchburg, VA.

Sutton, Joseph J. *2nd West Virginia Cavalry.* 2001 Reprint. Blue Acorn Press, Huntington, WVA.

Walker, Gary C. *Hunter's Fiery Raid Through Virginia Valleys.* 1989. A. W. Enterprise. Roanoke, VA.

Wise, Jennings C. *Virginia Military Institute: Military History.* 1915. J. P. Bell. Lynchburg, VA.

Woodward, Harold R. *Defender of the Valley: Brigadier General John David Imboden, CSA.* 1996. Rockbridge Publishing Co., Berryville, VA.

INDEX

AUTHOR SKETCH

Van Naisawald, a history lover all his life, has combined this love of history with military service as an artillery officer, a military history writing career that includes three prior books on the Civil War, a book on WWII, and many magazine historical articles. A graduate of both VMI and UNC, Naisawald is a retired lieutenant colonel and former army historian, speechwriter and magazine editor for the Army. He currently resides in Lynchburg, Virginia, and is a member of the Advisory Board of Historic Sandusky.